AMERICA'S PIONEER
JEWISH
CONGREGATIONS

AMERICA'S PIONEER JEWISH CONGREGATIONS

ARCHITECTURE, COMMUNITY AND HISTORY

JULIAN H. PREISLER

FONTHILL

This book is dedicated to the generations before us and those yet to come. Our history is amazing and it is always being created, thus we must continue to record and preserve it. I thank my family for their patience and for always encouraging me to do the work that I love. A special dedication goes to my mother, Dorothy Goldman Preisler (of blessed memory zl'), who passed away in 2015. Her support was constant and she would be so pleased to know that this particular book came to fruition.

Fonthill Media Language Policy

Fonthill Media publishes in the international English language market. One language edition is published worldwide. As there are minor differences in spelling and presentation, especially with regard to American English and British English, a policy is necessary to define which form of English to use. The Fonthill Policy is to use the form of English native to the author. Julian H. Preisler was born and educated in the United States of America, and therefore American English has been adopted in this publication.

Fonthill Media Limited
Fonthill Media LLC
www.fonthillmedia.com
office@fonthillmedia.com

First published in the United Kingdom and the United States of America 2017

British Library Cataloguing in Publication Data:
A catalogue record for this book is available from the British Library

Copyright © Julian H. Preisler 2017

ISBN 978-1-62545-037-1

The right of Julian H. Preisler to be identified as the author of this work has been asserted by him in accordance with the Copyright, Designs and Patents Act 1988.

Typeset in 10pt on 13pt Sabon
Printed and bound by CPI Group (UK) Ltd, Croydon, CR0 4YY

Foreword

Rabbi Elliot Gertel—Rabbi Emeritus: Congregation Rodfei Zedek, Chicago Julian H. Preisler's work has opened up the world of American Judaism in unique, artistic and engaging ways. Over the past several years, he has offered memorable glimpses into American synagogue history and architecture through photographs and the printed page, always utilizing newer media as they developed, including CDs and the internet. I think especially of his 2008 eBook, *American Synagogues: A Photographic Journey*. In multiple media, he has made synagogue building gems, many in remote outposts, accessible to people who might never have seen them and who could not have found them pictured in existing books.

With *America's Pioneer Jewish Congregations*, Preisler returns to the printed and photograph genres, and continues, with heartfelt words and inviting pictures, to stir and inspire us to familiarize ourselves with the beauty of modernistic and classic synagogue facades and interiors, and, above all, with the dedication and faith of those who built those synagogues and remained devoted to them.

This book comes at a time of renewed interest in synagogue architecture representing various periods and persuasions in American Jewish life. This book's stories of the pioneers, along with the locales, including Puerto Rico and the United States Virgin Islands, are captivating invitations to explore a precious heritage and hopefully to bring new life to local historic congregations in city and country alike. Equally important, this book serves as a challenge and admonition to Jewish communities to preserve their architectural heirlooms, even if that means making sure that other congregations or organizations that purchase these buildings maintain major elements of the interiors and exteriors.

Thanks to Julian Preisler, I have, through the years, seen pictures of synagogues that I may not have otherwise beheld. As a synagogue architecture enthusiast, and as an avid student of American Jewish history, I am, as always, grateful to him for his efforts, and for his chronicling and preserving and illustrating what was achieved and prized by those who came before so that those who follow will find a standard and hopefully a groove and a memorable sojourn in places that can yet inspire those who would build the future of our Jewish community and of our country.

Acknowledgments

A book like this takes enormous time and effort to bring together and an undertaking such as this would not be possible without the interest and enthusiasm of the congregations featured as well as historical societies, and archives that provided many of the fascinating images. Thankfully there were few congregations that, for some reason, would not provide photographs or information. I would like to thank all the congregations and their staff and members who provided me with information and photographs. A special thank you is extended to the following people and institutions especially cooperative in bringing this project to fruition: Susan Thomas (Spring Hill Avenue Temple: Mobile, Alabama); Larry Steinberg (Temple Emanuel: Honolulu, Hawaii); Fredric Stein Photography (Chicago, Illinois); Richard Edelman (Barnert Temple: Franklin Lakes, New Jersey); Beverly Tetterton (Temple of Israel: Wilmington, North Carolina); Susan Donchin & Andrew Feiler Photography (B'nai Israel: Oklahoma City, Oklahoma); Henry Kunowski and Joshua Kashinsky (Beth Israel: Portland, Oregon); Louis Kessler (Mikveh Israel: Philadelphia, Pennsylvania); Judy Weidman (Beth Israel: Houston, Texas); Stella Minion, Toes In The Sand Photography (Hebrew Congregation of St. Thomas, USVI); Miriam C. Mayer, PhD. (Ohavi Zedek: Burlington, Vermont); Sharon Beltz & Larry Grossman (Temple Beth Shalom: Spokane, Washington); Samuel D. Gruber; Jay Hyland (Jewish Museum Milwaukee); Alyssa Neely & Dale Rosengarten (College of Charleston Library); A huge thank you goes to Richard W. Clark for his insights and photograph editing knowledge.

Introduction

Our American Jewish Community is diverse, historic and the second largest in the world. It is always growing and changing. This is one reason why documentation is so important. This book takes as its purpose the identification and documentation of the oldest existing Jewish congregation in each of the 50 US States; Washington, DC; Puerto Rico; and the US Virgin Islands. My goal was to provide an informal introduction to the history of each congregation and to showcase the synagogue buildings in use over the years. It is not meant to be an in-depth look at each congregation and as with books such as this one, photograph and text limits are always a consideration. All the information contained in the book is correct to the best of my knowledge.

his book is part history, travel guide and photograph collection. Many of the vintage images have never appeared in a publication intended for a wide-reaching audience and help tell the story of the beginnings of organized Jewish religious life all over the country.

So why is a book like this important? My interest in history and synagogue architecture goes back nearly 30 years. Buildings fascinate me, and I am drawn to synagogues. This is my passion and it is vital that we document our "built" Jewish environment and share what we find. Placing importance on our past is as vital as the time and energy given to the present and future of our communities.

ALABAMA

Springhill Avenue Temple—Congregation Sha'arai Shomayim

The first permanent Jewish settlement in Alabama was in Mobile in the 1820s, with more Jewish residents arriving in the 1830s. By 1841 Jewish families organized and purchased land for a Jewish cemetery. Congregation Sha'arai Shomayim, whose original name translates as "Gates of Heaven and Society of Friends of the Needy," was incorporated in 1844.

The first synagogue in the state was dedicated in 1846 on St. Emanuel Street between Government and Church Streets. In 1850, the old Musical Association Hall was purchased for a new synagogue. The congregation outgrew the building and in 1853 a former church on Jackson Street between St. Louis and St. Michael's Streets was dedicated. The building burned in 1856 and was rebuilt in 1858 in the Greek Revival style. The Ten Commandments tablets from the 1858 synagogue are housed in the present temple.

In 1878, Congregation Sha'arai Shomayim was one of the earliest congregations in the country to join what is now the Union for Reform Judaism.

In 1907, elaborate services were held to dedicate a magnificent new temple on the corner of Government and Warren Streets. The Romanesque Revival style temple had beautiful stained glass windows and two domed towers. Known as the *Government Street Temple*, it was in use for over five decades. The pulpit menorahs and replica stained glass windows from the 1907 building are housed in the present temple.

In 1952, it was decided to sell the Government Street building and plan for a modern and larger synagogue. Members were moving from the area and the building was difficult and expensive to repair. The new temple was dedicated in 1955. It is known as the *Spring Hill Avenue Temple*, reflecting its location at 1769 Spring Hill Avenue. The design by T. Cooper Van Antwerp was acclaimed as one of Mobile's most beautiful buildings and was awarded for outstanding architecture and design by the Historic Mobile Preservation Society.

In 1999, ground was broken for a new chapel and addition. None of the previous synagogue buildings survive, but a historical marker exists at the site of the 1907 synagogue at 565 Government Street, marking the early history of the congregation.

The original Jewish cemetery was purchased in 1841 as a distinct portion of the Magnolia Cemetery. This cemetery was used until 1876 when the "New Jewish Cemetery" was dedicated on Owens Streets.

Mobile, Alabama: Spring Hill Avenue Temple—View of the front of the present temple, 2008; Courtesy Author's Collection.

Mobile, Alabama: Spring Hill Avenue Temple—View of the bimah & Ark in the Main Sanctuary, n.d.; Courtesy of the Spring Hill Avenue Temple.

Mobile, Alabama: Spring Hill Avenue Temple—Exterior of the Government Street Temple, ca 1915; Courtesy of Library of Congress, Prints & Photographs Division, LC-DIG-det-4a23643.

Mobile, Alabama: Spring Hill Avenue Temple—Interior of the Government Street Temple, n.d. Courtesy of the Spring Hill Avenue Temple.

Right: Mobile, Alabama: Spring Hill Avenue Temple—Exterior of the Jackson Street Temple, n.d.; Courtesy of the Spring Hill Avenue Temple.

Below: Mobile, Alabama: Spring Hill Avenue Temple—Sanctuary interior of the Jackson Street Temple, n.d.; Courtesy of the Spring Hill Avenue Temple.

ALASKA

Congregation Beth Sholom

The 49th State has one of the youngest organized Jewish communities in the country. Despite this fact, Jews have been a prominent part of Alaska's history for over 140 years.

Alaska's first formal Jewish community began in 1900 with the founding of the Nome Hebrew Congregation, which disbanded after World War One. There are historic Jewish cemeteries in Fairbanks (1906) and Dawson City-Klondike (1902). Congregation Bikkur Cholim was formally organized in 1908 in Fairbanks, but also no longer exists. In 1980, the Jewish Congregation of Fairbanks was incorporated and in 1992 became Congregation Or Ha Tzafon.

The state's oldest continuous Jewish congregation is Beth Sholom, formed in 1958 in Anchorage. In 1960, the congregation affiliated with what is now the Union of Reform Judaism. Anchorage has the largest concentration of Jewish residents in the state.

The first home for Beth Sholom was built in 1965 and located at 1000 20th Avenue. It was a simple structure, but was the first purpose built synagogue in the state. As the congregation grew a new synagogue complex was completed in 1988 at 7525 East Northern Lights Boulevard. The facilities were recently renovated and expanded. A Beth Sholom section exists at the Anchorage Memorial Park Cemetery

Anchorage, Alaska: Congregation Beth Sholom—View of the present renovated and expanded synagogue, 2016; Courtesy of Congregation Beth Sholom.

ARIZONA

Temple Emanu-El

Jews are known to have lived in what is now Arizona as early as the mid-1800s when gold was discovered. Herbert Arizona Drachman is noted as the first Caucasian male born in the Arizona Territory in 1869 in Tucson.

It was not until 1910, however, that the first enduring Jewish congregation, Temple Emanu-El, was organized and officially chartered as the Hebrew Benevolent Society. The earlier Tombstone Hebrew Congregation, formed in 1861, only lasted about ten years.

Temple Emanu-El built the first synagogue in the Territory in use from 1910 to 1949 and designated a historic landmark in 1982. Located at 560 Stone Avenue and always known as the *Stone Avenue Temple*, even after it was no longer in use as a synagogue. After a complete restoration and expansion, it is presently known as the Jewish Heritage Museum and Holocaust Center.

By 1940, the Stone Avenue Temple building could no longer serve the growing congregation. A campaign to raise funds for a larger synagogue was interrupted by the war, but plans began again in 1948. The first unit of the synagogue complex at 225 North Country Club Road was a multi-purpose auditorium dedicated in 1949. A new wing with chapel, library, offices, etc. was completed in 1959. The large sanctuary and religious school was completed in 1962. A formal dedication for the entire synagogue complex, which took thirteen years to complete, was held in 1963. The congregation is noted for its sanctuary, and also the Biblical Garden. A large preschool building was built in 2000. Temple Emanu-El is a member of the Union for Reform Judaism.

The congregation owns a section of the Evergreen Memorial Park Cemetery on Oracle Road in Tucson; the Shaarai Shalom section of the All Faiths Memorial Park on S. Avenida Los Reyes also in Tucson and the Temple Emanu-El Cemetery in Nogales at Cemetery Street West. The Nogales cemetery is an "affiliate" cemetery of Temple Emanu-El and is privately owned.

Jewish Church, 17th and Stone Ave., Tucson, Arizona.

Above: Tucson, Arizona: Temple Emanu-El—Exterior of present temple; 2007, Courtesy of the Author's Collection.

Opposite above: Tucson, Arizona: Temple Emanu-El—Exterior of the Stone Avenue Temple, 2007; Courtesy of the Author's Collection.

Opposite below: Tucson, Arizona: Temple Emanu-El—Vintage postcard of the Stone Avenue Temple; ca. 1910- 1919; Courtesy of Special Collections, College of Charleston Libraries.

ARKANSAS

Congregation B'nai Israel & Temple Anshe Emeth

German Jewish settlers arrived in Arkansas during the 1840s and 1850s, and the 1880s brought significant numbers of Eastern European Jews to the state.

The Jewish congregations in Pine Bluff and Little Rock were both formed in 1866 and chartered in 1867. Anshe Emeth in Pine Bluff was chartered first and B'nai Israel in Little Rock was chartered five days later. In 1867, Anshe Emeth dedicated its first synagogue. The congregation existed until 2016 when the last religious service was held and the congregation was formally closed. Two of their three synagogues still stand in Pine Bluff, the 1902 and 1967 temples, as well as the Jewish Cemetery section of Bellwood Cemetery.

Congregation B'nai Israel in Little Rock is now the oldest existing Jewish congregation in the state. It began informally in 1866 and was chartered in 1867 as Congregation Children of Israel. The first temple was dedicated in 1872 on Center Street between Third and Fourth Streets. It was a small brick structure that soon outgrew the congregation. A new temple was dedicated in 1897 by the founder of the American Reform movement, Bohemian-born Rabbi Isaac Mayer Wise.

The Romanesque Revival style temple was located at Capitol Street and Broadway. Prominent features included a circular double dome, large clock tower and a colonnade. The sanctuary interior contained a domed ceiling and stained glass windows. An annex was built in 1949.

B'nai Israel began as an Orthodox congregation, but in 1872 adopted the American Reform prayer book, and in 1873 became a charter member of today's Union for Reform Judaism.

The current temple on Rodney Parham Road is in suburban Little Rock. Dedicated in 1975, the structure is contemporary in design, using extensive amounts of glass, allowing natural light into the sanctuary. The old Capitol Street temple no longer stands. Many of the furnishings and artifacts from it were moved to the new temple, which was completely renovated in 2008.

B'nai Israel has a section at Oakland Cemetery on Barber Avenue in East Little Rock, dedicated in 1875. Mount Holly Cemetery once had a Jewish section established by Morris Navra, one of the founders of B'nai Israel. The Jewish burial ground was governed by the Arkansas Jewish Burial Society, formed in 1860. The section initially served as the burial ground for Navra's daughter, but was expanded to serve as the "Israelite Burying Ground." All of the graves were eventually moved to the Oakland Cemetery.

Above: Pine Bluff, Arkansas: Temple Anshe Emeth—Exterior of the former 2nd Avenue & Poplar Street temple, 2007; Courtesy of the Author's Collection

Right: Little Rock, Arkansas: Congregation B'nai Israel—Exterior of the Capitol Street temple, n.d. Courtesy of Congregation B'nai Israel.

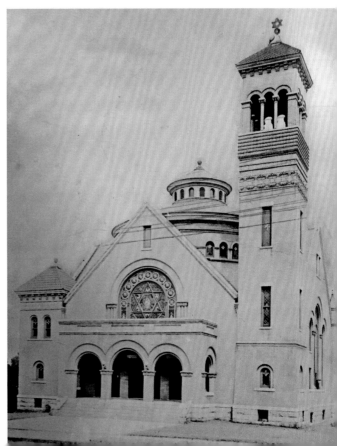

CALIFORNIA

Sherith Israel & Temple Emanu-El, San Francisco; Temple Israel, Stockton

Three distinct Jewish congregations are featured for California because of their nearly simultaneous beginnings. Emanu-El and Sherith Israel trace their beginnings to 1849, when observances of the High Holy Days were held. Emanu-El Congregation was established in 1850. Because of preferences concerning religious ritual, it was decided to have a congregation following the Ashkenazic German ritual and one following the Polish ritual.

Emanu-El became the German ritual congregation. The first synagogue of Emanu-El was dedicated in 1854 on Broadway between Powell and Mason. The congregation and the Jewish community expanded rapidly during the latter half of the 19th century, and this led to the need for a larger synagogue. A new temple at 450 Sutter Street was dedicated in 1866. The Gothic Revival style structure had twin towers capped with small bronze plated domes. It received extensive damage during the earthquake of 1906, but was rebuilt and served for twenty more years.

Congregation Emanu-El began as an Orthodox congregation, but by 1877, the congregation had embraced the Reform movement and became a member of today's Union for Reform Judaism. In 1926, the current Mediterranean Revival facility was dedicated and is located at Arguello Boulevard and Lake Street. A unique feature is the tile covered dome over the main sanctuary.

The first Emanu-El cemetery was established in 1850 at Vallejo and Gough Streets. In 1860, a burial ground was purchased at Eighteenth and Dolores in the Mission District. This cemetery became known as the Home of Peace Cemetery and served for nearly 30 years. It was totally destroyed in the earthquake and fire of 1906. The current cemetery of Emanu-El is at 1299 El Camino Real in Colma.

Congregation Sherith Israel was formed by those early Jews who preferred the Polish ritual worship service. A temporary congregation was formed in April 1850. In August 1850, a permanent congregation was established. The first synagogue for the congregation was dedicated in 1854 on Stockton Street, between Broadway and Vallejo. A second synagogue was dedicated in 1870 at Post and Taylor. The congregation now worships in its third structure located at California and Webster Streets. The cornerstone of this historic structure was laid in 1904. Sherith Israel's synagogue was one of the few public buildings to survive the great earthquake and fire of 1906. The interior design has intricately carved woodwork, Italian stained glass windows, and a rich and varied palate of colors. Renovation projects to the structure have recently been completed.

Sherith Israel maintains the Hills of Eternity Memorial Park at 1301 El Camino Boulevard in Colma. Also maintained are Portals of Eternity and Gardens of Eternity. This cemetery complex was founded in 1851 and incorporated in 1860 as "Giboth Olam." The first Jewish cemetery at Vallejo and Gough Streets, established in 1850, was cared for by both Sherith Israel and Emanu-El. Sherith Israel also had a cemetery adjoining the Emanu-El ground at Eighteenth and Dolores.

Temple Israel of Stockton began late in 1849 with the formation of the benevolent society Ryhim Ahoovim. The group became a congregation by 1855. Their first synagogue was completed in 1855 on Miner Avenue, between Hunter and El Dorado

Streets. Eight years later the synagogue was moved to a new location at Hunter Street, between Lindsay and Fremont. In 1892, a change from the Orthodox ritual to the Reform ritual became official. In 1906 Temple Israel, as it was now known, became a member of today's Union for Reform Judaism.

In 1905, a new temple was dedicated on Hunter Street with the old synagogue used for the religious school. The 1905 synagogue was moved in 1930 to Madison and Willow Streets adjoining the new Jewish Community Center. A few years later the old synagogue was moved to American Street and a new synagogue was built next to the Jewish Community Center. The new Moorish Revival synagogue had a dome, twin towers and a stained glass window above the entrance. It no longer stands, but the former Jewish Community Center building similar in style to the synagogue still stands, as does the 1855 synagogue now a residence. In 1960 land was purchased at El Dorado Street and March Lane and classrooms were built, then offices, and in 1972, a sanctuary was dedicated. Temple Israel's 1851 cemetery is the oldest Jewish cemetery west of the Rocky Mountains.

San Francisco, California: Congregation Emanu-El—Exterior of Sutter Street temple; 1866; Courtesy of the Library of Congress, Prints & Photographs Division, LC-USZ62-28152.

Left: San Francisco, California: Congregation Emanu-El— Postcard of present temple complex, ca. 1960's; Courtesy of the Author's Collection

Below: San Francisco, California: Congregation Emanu-El—Sanctuary interior of the present temple, 2016; Courtesy of Congregation Emanu-El.

Above: San Francisco, California: Congregation Sherith Israel—Exterior view of present synagogue, 2007; Courtesy of the Author's Collection

Right: San Francisco, California: Congregation Sherith Israel—Exterior view of present synagogue, 2007; Courtesy of the Author's Collection.

Above left: Stockton, California: Temple Israel—Exterior of first synagogue on Miner Avenue (later moved to Hunter Street, n.d.; Courtesy of the Western States Jewish History Association WS0790-6-N

Above right: Stockton, California: Temple Israel—Exterior of the 1905 synagogue on Hunter Street, n.d.; Courtesy of the Western States Jewish History Association WS1926-13-N

Opposite above: Stockton, California: Temple Israel—Sanctuary interior of the 1905 synagogue on Hunter Street, n.d.; Courtesy of the Western States Jewish History Association WS1798-12-N

Opposite below: Stockton, California: Temple Israel—Exterior of the synagogue on Madison and Willow Streets, n.d.; Courtesy of the Western States Jewish History Association WS1929-13-N

COLORADO

Temple Emanuel

Denver is home to the oldest Jewish congregation in Colorado. Denver had enough Jewish residents by 1859 to hold the first High Holy Days services in Colorado. Temple Emanuel's beginnings were in a prayer and burial society formed in 1866. The congregation was formally incorporated in 1874.

Their first synagogue was located at 19th and Curtis Streets and was dedicated in 1875. In 1882 Temple Emanuel dedicated a larger synagogue located at 24th and Curtis Streets. After a fire gutted this synagogue in 1897 (the building still stands today and is used as artist space and home to several bakeries), Temple Emanuel built again, this time uptown at 16th and Pearl Streets. This synagogue was dedicated in 1899. Designed with Moorish and Byzantine features it has two domed towers plus four additional domes. The facility was expanded in the 1920s, but by the early 1950s, the process of building a larger and modern synagogue began.

The present synagogue complex on Grape Street was completed in two stages with the social hall and school ready for use by 1957. The large mid-century modern style sanctuary is fan-shaped with a gabled roof. A cupola in the center is in the shape of a Torah crown. It was dedicated in 1960 and designed by Percival Goodman, who designed over 50 synagogues. An expansion and renovation project was completed in 1987. The synagogue's chapel contains many furnishings from the Pearl Street temple as well as furnishings, artifacts and the Torah from the synagogue that once existed in Kolin, Czechoslovakia, destroyed by the Nazis.

Temple Emanuel's first burial ground, a section of the City Cemetery, was used from 1859 to 1890. The second cemetery for the congregation is a section of Riverside Cemetery at East 52nd Avenue and Race Street. It was in use from 1896 to 1911. The third and current cemetery was established in 1911 in a section of Fairmount Cemetery at 430 South Quebec Street.

Denver, Colorado: Temple Emanuel—Exterior of present Grape Street temple; Courtesy of Louis Davidson Synagogues360.com

24

Denver, Colorado: Temple Emanuel—Vintage postcard of the Pearl Street temple, n.d.; Courtesy of Special Collections, College of Charleston Libraries.

Denver, Colorado: Temple Emanuel—Exterior of the former temple at Curtis & 24th Streets, 2009, Courtesy of Wikimedia Commons User: MidMacMan.

CONNECTICUT

Congregation Mishkan Israel and Congregation Beth Israel

Both Congregation Mishkan Israel in Hamden and Congregation Beth Israel in West Hartford were the first official Jewish congregations established in the state in 1843. This was the year the Connecticut law prohibiting the formation of non-Christian societies was rescinded.

German Jews in New Haven assembled for worship as early as 1840 and began a group with no official recognition until 1843. Mishkan Israel's first permanent synagogue was a former church on Court Street acquired in 1856 and used for over 40 years. By 1895 Mishkan Israel broke ground for their first purpose-built synagogue. The new temple at Audubon and Orange Streets was dedicated in 1897. Designed by Arnold Brunner with Classical, Italianate and Colonial influences, the building features two 84-foot-high towers and is now used as a performing arts center. Its style has also been called Spanish Renaissance.

The congregation was Reform in its worship as early as 1856 and became an early member of today's Union for Reform Judaism. By the 1950s the congregation had outgrown the Audubon Street temple. Property in suburban Hamden on Ridge Road was purchased in 1955 and by 1960 the congregation had moved into its new temple. Designed by the noted architect and German-Jewish refugee Fritz Nathan, it features an Ark set into a semicircular wall with floor to ceiling stained glass windows and a 25-foot-high mosaic Decalogue.

Mishkan Israel's cemetery dates to 1843 and many of the earliest Jews of New Haven are buried there. It is located in the Westville Section of the city at the corner of Whalley Avenue and Jewell Street.

Beth Israel in West Hartford was officially formed in 1843, but the group may have met for worship as early as 1839. The congregation began in Hartford as an Orthodox congregation, but soon instituted many reforms and in 1877 became one of the founding members of today's Union for Reform Judaism.

Their first building at 942 Main Street was a former church. Their first purpose-built synagogue and the first in Connecticut was dedicated in 1876 at 21 Charter Oak Avenue. The style is Eclectic with Gothic, Romanesque and Moorish influences. In 1898, the building was enlarged and renovated. Beth Israel moved to its present site on Farmington Avenue in West Hartford in 1936. The landmark status domed building is in the Byzantine Revival style softened with Art Deco influences. In 2006 Beth Israel was given the West Hartford Historic Preservation Award for its meticulous restoration. The Goldfarb Community Learning Center opened in 2008 featuring the library, media center, museum and archives.

Beth Israel has two cemeteries, the 1855 burial ground on Affleck Street in Hartford and a newer cemetery in Avon on Jackson Street.

New Haven, Connecticut: Congregation Mishkan Israel—Vintage postcard of the Audubon and Orange Streets temple, 1905; Courtesy of Special Collections, College of Charleston Libraries.

Hamden, Connecticut: Congregation Mishkan Israel—Exterior of the present temple, n.d.; Courtesy of Samuel D. Gruber—Jewish Art & Monuments Blog.

Above: Hamden, Connecticut: Congregation Mishkan Israel—Sanctuary interior of the present temple, n.d.; Courtesy of Samuel D. Gruber—Jewish Art & Monuments Blog.

Left: Hartford, Connecticut: Congregation Beth Israel—Exterior of the former Charter Oak Avenue temple, 2010; Courtesy of Wikimedia Commons User: Grondemar.

28

Above: West Hartford, Connecticut: Congregation Beth Israel—Exterior of the present temple, 2008; Courtesy of Congregation Beth Israel.

Right: West Hartford, Connecticut: Congregation Beth Israel—Sanctuary interior of the present temple, 2008; Courtesy of Congregation Beth Israel.

DELAWARE

Congregation Adas Kodesch Shel Emeth

Of the thirteen original colonies, Delaware was the second after New York to permit Jews to be admitted legally, but it was not until 1883 that the Montefiore Society was legally incorporated, thus becoming the first and oldest official Jewish organization in Delaware.

The first congregation, Ohabe Shalom, began in 1880, but lasted only a few years. In 1885, the first enduring congregation, Adas Kodesch, was founded and formally organized in 1889, as the Orthodox Adas Kodesch Congregation.

In 1898, its first permanent space was acquired by purchasing a former church at Sixth & French Streets. The congregation grew and a new synagogue was built in 1908 on the same site. It was a unique building in Wilmington with its twin domed towers.

Adas Kodesch grew and, by the mid-1950s, the need to build a larger synagogue and school was evident. In 1957, the Chesed Shel Emeth Congregation and the Adas Kodesch Congregation merged. Chesed Shel Emeth, also Orthodox, was founded in 1901, but used the Sephardic ritual for worship. Their synagogue was dedicated in 1915 at Third and Shipley Streets. The merged congregation, Adas Kodesch Shel Emeth, dedicated its new facility in 1963 designed by the noted American synagogue architect, Percival Goodman. It is located at Washington Street Extension and Torah Drive in the Brandywine Hills section of the city.

The synagogue was designed in a modern rustic style with extensive use of brick and wood characteristic of many of Goodman's synagogues. The congregation follows the Traditional ritual today and began "modernizing" their Orthodox form of worship in the 1940s.

The Adas Kodesch Shel Emeth Section of the Jewish Community Cemetery on Foulk Road in Wilmington was purchased in1890 from the Lombardy Cemetery Company. The present burial ground is a merger of the Adas Kodesch and Shel Emeth sections. An earlier Jewish cemetery at 5th & Hawley Streets was established by the Montefiore Society in 1886. In 1910 Adas Kodesch purchased additional land at their cemetery and moved the bodies from the 1886 cemetery and sold the property.

Opposite above: Wilmington, Delaware: Adas Kodesch Shel Emeth—Exterior of the French Street synagogue, 1941; Courtesy of the Jewish Historical Society of Delaware.

Opposite below: Wilmington, Delaware: Adas Kodesch Shel Emeth—Sanctuary interior of the French Street synagogue, 1941; Courtesy of the Jewish Historical Society of Delaware.

Above: Wilmington, Delaware: Adas Kodesch Shel Emeth—Exterior of Chesed Shel Emeth's Third & Shipley Streets synagogue, 1930's; Courtesy of Jewish Historical Society of Delaware.

Below: Wilmington, Delaware: Adas Kodesch Shel Emeth—Facade of the present synagogue, 2008; Courtesy of Debra Steinberg.

DISTRICT OF COLUMBIA

Washington Hebrew Congregation

The first Jewish congregation in the Nation's Capital was the Washington Hebrew Congregation founded in 1852 and issued a charter by Congress in 1857 when legislation was enacted that gave the congregation full equality with the churches in the city. In 1863, the congregation purchased a former church on 8th Street, NW between H and I Streets. The first purpose-built synagogue was dedicated in 1898 on the same site. The cornerstone laying ceremony included participation of then President William McKinley, his Cabinet and many Christian clergy.

The new synagogue was an imposing Moorish Revival structure with a central dome and two domed towers. It still stands and is home to a church. Less than fifteen years after the building's dedication the congregation was already experiencing growing pains. No action was taken for a number of years and soon the depression and the war years diverted the attention of the members and the leadership. It was not until the early 1950s that land was purchased at Macomb Street and Massachusetts Avenue and plans were drawn up for a new synagogue. The cornerstone of the synagogue was laid in 1952, with then President Harry S. Truman as speaker for the ceremony. The synagogue was dedicated in 1955 and the main address was given by then President Dwight D. Eisenhower.

The structure is Mid-Century Modern in style with a sweeping rounded end and marble columned entrance. The main sanctuary contains large white marble Ten Commandments as the Ark doors as well as a large stained glass wall. A suburban campus was later established in suburban Potomac, Maryland.

Washington Hebrew Congregation's cemetery was established around 1879 on Alabama Avenue, Southeast. It was begun after an earlier cemetery on Hamilton Road was closed and the burials were transferred to the Alabama Avenue location. In 2000, the Garden of Remembrance was opened in Clarksburg, Maryland. Washington Hebrew was instrumental in forming the first not-for-profit Jewish cemetery in the region.

Above: Washington, District of Columbia: Washington Hebrew Congregation—Facade and entrance of the present temple, 2008; Courtesy of Washington Hebrew Congregation.

Below: Washington, District of Columbia: Washington Hebrew Congregation—Sanctuary interior of the present temple, 2008; Courtesy of Washington Hebrew Congregation.

Right: Washington, District of Columbia: Washington Hebrew Congregation—Facade of the former 8th & I Streets temple, 2015; Courtesy of the Author's Collection

Below: Washington, District of Columbia: Washington Hebrew Congregation—View of the former 8th and I Streets temple taken from H & 9th Streets, ca. 1940; Courtesy of the Library of Congress Prints & Photographs Division. LC-USW3-038152-E

FLORIDA

Temple Beth El

Colonial Florida was not always hospitable to the settlement of Jews. However, prior to Florida becoming a United States territory, Jews lived and owned land and businesses in such places as Pensacola, St. Augustine, and Tallahassee.

The first Jewish institution was formed in Jacksonville in 1857, when the Jacksonville Hebrew Cemetery came into being. But it was not until 1876 when the state's first congregation was organized as the Reform Temple Beth El in Pensacola and chartered in 1878.

The congregation built its first synagogue at 37 East Chase Street. The building was destroyed by fire in 1895 and was quickly replaced by a brick structure on the same site that was dedicated in 1896. In 1889, the Beth El joined the Reform movement.

The temple was again destroyed by fire in December of 1929. A number of items, including the Ten Commandments tablets and organ, were salvaged and included in the new synagogue built at the corner of Palafox and Cervantes Streets. The Art Deco synagogue was dedicated in 1931. An Education Wing was built in 1960. The synagogue was recently restored and expanded.

The Beth El Cemetery is on Cervantes Street between Q and R Streets and was established in 1876, when Sam Goldbach donated the land. It is the third oldest Jewish cemetery in Florida.

Pensacola, Florida: Temple Beth El—Exterior of the present temple, 2016; Courtesy of Chuck Lisner Photography and Temple Beth El.

Pensacola, Florida: Temple Beth El—Sanctuary interior of the present temple, 2016; Courtesy of Chuck Lisner Photography and Temple Beth El.

Pensacola, Florida: Temple Beth El—New addition to the present temple, 2016; Courtesy of Chuck Lisner Photography and Temple Beth El.

Above: Pensacola, Florida: Temple Beth El—Exterior of the second temple on East Chase Street, ca. 1896; Courtesy of the Florida Jewish Museum and Marcia Jo Zerivitz.

Below: Pensacola, Florida: Temple Beth El—Exterior of the second temple on East Chase Street after renovations, 1905; Courtesy of the Florida Jewish Museum and Marcia Jo Zerivitz.

GEORGIA

Congregation Mickve Israel

The first Jews in Georgia landed in Savannah 1733, from London, England. These individuals were mainly Sephardic Jews and in 1735 they formed the first Jewish congregation in Georgia, Kahal Kodesh Mickve Israel or Holy Congregation Hope of Israel.

Other Jewish colonists began settling in Savannah, but by 1740 only a few remained in Savannah. The war between Spain and England had reached the shores of Georgia and many in the largely Sephardic community fled north to Charleston, South Carolina. They were fearful of the Spanish Church which viewed the Sephardic Jews as apostates, which was punishable by death.

The Jews who fled returned to Savannah and the rejuvenated congregation was granted a charter in 1790. Mickve Israel is one of six congregations from America's Colonial period.

The first synagogue in the state was built at Perry Lane and Whitaker Street in 1820. This frame structure was destroyed by fire in 1829, and a new brick building was dedicated in 1841 on the same site. The congregation remained Sephardic in ritual, but moved slowly toward Reform Judaism and in 1904 became a member of the Reform movement.

As growth continued, a new and larger building was constructed to meet the needs of the congregation. In 1878, the present Monterey Square Temple on Bull Street was consecrated. The structure was designed by the English architect Henry G. Harrison in a pure Gothic architectural style, complete with apse, transept, vaulted ceilings, and stained glass windows. It is unique among American synagogues America. The Mordecai Sheftall Memorial building was added in 1902, expanded in 1957 and rebuilt in 2003. It houses the museum, school and offices.

The first Jewish burial ground in Georgia was at the present median strip at Oglethorpe Street, west of Bull Street, and was established in 1733. The Jewish Community Cemetery, aka Mordecai Sheftall Cemetery, on Broughton Street began about 1769 with the last burial taking place in 1881. It is also called the "Old Hebrew Burying Ground." In 1853, a section of the Laurel Grove Cemetery was purchased and a section of Bonaventure Cemetery was purchased in 1909.

Above: Savannah, Georgia: Congregation Mickve Israel—Sketch by Milton Kassell of what the 1841 temple is thought to have looked like, 1966; Courtesy of Congregation Mickve Israel

Left: Savannah, Georgia: Congregation Mickve Israel—Front view of the present temple, 1960's; Courtesy of the Library of Congress Prints & Photographs Division, HABS, GA,26- SAV,76--1

Above: Savannah, Georgia: Congregation Mickve Israel—Side view of the present temple, 1960's; Courtesy of the Library of Congress Prints & Photographs Division, HABS, GA,26-SAV,76--2

Below: Savannah, Georgia: Congregation Mickve Israel—Sanctuary interior of the present temple, ca. 2016; Courtesy of Congregation Mickve Israel.

HAWAII

Temple Emanu-El

The Hawaiian Islands have had Jewish settlers since the 1850s when German Jews began arriving in the Kingdom. When Hawaii was annexed to the United States in 1898, the Jewish population was approximately 200 adults.

The first public Jewish religious services were held in 1898. In 1901, the First Hebrew Congregation of Honolulu was established but lasted only until 1907 when it disbanded. Public religious services and a communal Seder were re-established in 1919, and in 1922 the Aloha Jewish Center was opened for the use of Jewish servicemen.

It was not until 1938 that the civilian Jewish population organized the Honolulu Jewish Community. A synagogue center in a converted chapel was dedicated in 1939. In 1946, the location was moved, and in 1948 the group's name was changed to Congregation of the Honolulu Jewish Community. In 1951, a large home was purchased for a synagogue. The Honolulu Jewish Congregation became Temple Emanu-El in 1951. The following year the temple affiliated with the Reform movement and officially adopted its new name.

The present Mid-Century Modern synagogue on Pali Highway was in dedicated in 1960. The complex includes many courts and gardens. The Ark is constructed as a teak-wood grill flanked by colored glass and walls of mahogany wood. Teak-wood is also used on the pulpit and choir screen. A Torah scroll and yad or pointer belonging to early Jewish resident, Elias Abraham Rosenberg, was given to King David Kalākaua of Hawaii for safekeeping in 1887 when Rosenberg left the island for San Francisco. These historical ritual items were eventually given to Temple Emanu-El and are on permanent display.

The first Jewish cemetery in Hawaii was dedicated in 1902 near Pearl City. Known as the Hebrew Cemetery, the land was appropriated by the United States Navy during World War Two. The Hebrew Burial Association was then formed in 1942 and purchased land in the Oahu Cemetery on Nuuanu Avenue in Honolulu. The cemetery title was transferred to Temple Emanu-El in 1955. Additional land was purchased in the Mililani Memorial Park Cemetery on Kamehameha Highway and the new Temple Emanu-El Cemetery was dedicated in 1974.

Above: Honolulu, Hawaii: Temple Emanu-El—Exterior of the present temple, 2016; Courtesy of Larry Steinberg and Temple Emanu-El.

Below: Honolulu, Hawaii: Temple Emanu-El—Vintage postcard of the present sanctuary interior, 1960's; Courtesy of Special Collections, College of Charleston Libraries.

Opposite: Honolulu, Hawaii: Temple Emanu-El—Original architectural rendering of the present temple, 1959; Courtesy of Larry Steinberg and Temple Emanu-El.

IDAHO

Congregation Ahavath Beth Israel

Pioneer Jewish families came to Idaho as early as 1861. The effort to establish a synagogue began in 1891 when Moses Alexander arrived in Boise. He and other leading Jewish citizens combined efforts to organize synagogue life, which resulted in the formation of Congregation Beth Israel in 1895. A lot at 11th and State Streets was purchased in May 1895, and in March 1896 the new synagogue was completed.

The building is Romanesque Revival in design with Moorish Revival influences. The sanctuary has large round arched clerestory windows and a circular rose window in the front facade. The building has a rough stone raised foundation and exterior walls covered with cedar shingles. The structure was restored in 1982. The building is the oldest synagogue building in continuous use west of the Mississippi River. Ahavath Israel was founded in Boise during the early 1900s by Jews with an Orthodox tradition of worship. Their own synagogue at 27th and Bannock Streets was built in 1948.

By 1986 efforts at a merger of the two congregation were completed. The former synagogue of Ahavath Israel is now used as photography studio. The historic 1896 synagogue was moved in 2003 from its original location to 11 North Latah Street to enable future expansion. Ahavath Beth Israel is a member of the Union for Reform Judaism.

The congregation's cemetery, Morris Hill Cemetery, was established in 1895. The City of Boise purchased a portion of the cemetery land that now serves as the city cemetery. The entire cemetery is referred to as Morris Hill Cemetery. A small non-Jewish cemetery known as the Pioneer Cemetery is located on Warm Springs Avenue and many pioneer Jewish families are buried there.

Boise, Idaho: Congregation Ahavath Beth Israel—Exterior of the present temple on its original State Street site, n.d.; Courtesy of the Library of Congress Prints & Photographs Division, HABS, ID,1-BOISE,11--1

Right: Boise, Idaho: Congregation Ahavath Beth Israel—Sanctuary interior of the present temple on its original State Street site, n.d.; Courtesy of the Library of Congress Prints and Photographs Division, HABS, ID,1-BOISE,11--4

Below: Boise, Idaho: Congregation Ahavath Beth Israel—Exterior of the present temple at its new Latah Street site, n.d.; Courtesy of Louis Davison Synagogues360.com

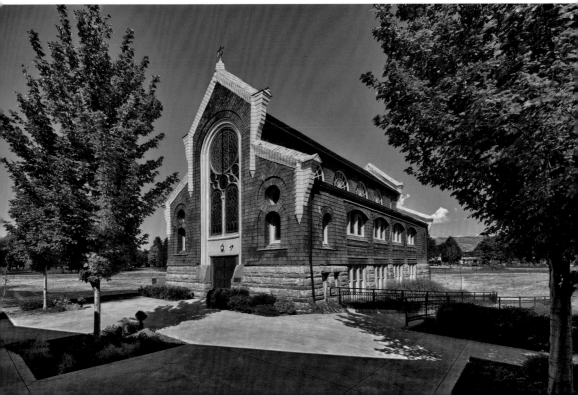

ILLINOIS

KAM Isaiah Israel Congregation

It was not until the 1830s that Jews began to settle in Chicago, and in 1845 the first Jewish religious service in the state was held. Kehilath Anshe Maarav, the first synagogue, was formed in 1847, in Chicago. The first synagogue to be built in Illinois was built for Kehilath Anshe Maarav in 1851 on Clark Street between Adams and Jackson Streets.

KAM Isaiah Israel Congregation today is composed of the following entities: Kehilath Anshe Maarav, B'nai Sholom, Temple Israel and Temple Isaiah. B'nai Sholom (1849) merged with Temple Israel (1894) to form B'nai Sholom Temple Israel in 1906. In 1923, they merged with Temple Isaiah (1895) to form Temple Isaiah Israel. This congregation, in turn, merged with Kehilath Anshe Maarav in 1971 to form the present-day congregation.

The congregation has had several locations and moved south with the Jewish community. Many of these structures still stand, but none are used for Jewish worship. In 1922, the congregation moved to 4945 South Drexel Boulevard and remained there until 1971 when the congregation merged with Temple Isaiah-Israel. The merged congregation, known now as KAM Isaiah Israel, worships in the Temple Isaiah-Israel building at 1100 South Hyde Park Blvd. The Hyde Park Boulevard building was constructed for the Isaiah Temple in 1923.

Designed by noted architect Alfred S. Altschuler, Sr. the octagonal Byzantine Revival structure features intricate brickwork, bas-relief carvings, a large central dome, and a minaret which serves a smoke stack. Stained glass windows, the dome, Italian marble Ark and colored mosaics are focal points. The chapel and Community Hall were completed in 1973 and there is a large museum on the premises.

KAM Isaiah Israel maintains several cemeteries. The Mount Isaiah Israel Cemetery is at 6600 West Addison Street. The Mount Mayriv Cemetery (part of Zion Gardens Cemetery) is at 3600 North Narragansett Avenue and the B'nai Sholom Section of Jewish Graceland Cemetery is at 3919 North Clark Street. The first Jewish cemetery in Illinois was established in 1845 on land that is now part of Lincoln Park on Chicago's North Side and was in use from 1845 to 1857.

Opposite above: Chicago, Illinois: KAM Isaiah Israel Congregation—Sketch by architect Dankmar Adler of the exterior of the Isaiah Temple at 45th Street and Vincennes Avenue, 1899; Courtesy of Author's Collection (*Chicago Daily Tribune* March 11, 1899)

Opposite below: Chicago, Illinois: KAM Isaiah Israel Congregation—Exterior of the former Kehilath Anshe Maarav synagogue on South Indiana Avenue, 1964; Courtesy of the Library of Congress Prints & Photographs Division, HABS, ILL,16-CHIG,56–1, Photographer: Harold Allen.

Above: Chicago, Illinois: KAM Isaiah Israel Congregation—Exterior of the former Kehilath Anshe Maarav synagogue on South Drexel Boulevard, 2016 Courtesy of Fredric Stein Photography.

Below left: Chicago, Illinois: KAM Isaiah Israel Congregation—Exterior of the present synagogue on South Hyde Park Boulevard, 2016; Courtesy of KAM Isaiah Israel Congregation and Fredric Stein Photography.

Below right: Chicago, Illinois: KAM Isaiah Israel Congregation—Exterior detail of the present synagogue on South Hyde Park Boulevard, 2016; Courtesy of KAM Isaiah Israel Congregation and Fredric Stein Photography.

Above: Chicago, Illinois: KAM Isaiah Israel Congregation—Entrance facade of the present synagogue on South Hyde Park Boulevard, 2016; Courtesy of KAM Isaiah Israel Congregation and Fredric Stein Photography.

Below: Chicago, Illinois: KAM Isaiah Israel Congregation—Sanctuary interior of the present synagogue on South Hyde Park Boulevard, 2016; Courtesy of KAM Isaiah Israel Congregation and Fredric Stein Photography.

INDIANA

Congregation Achduth VeSholom

Achduth Vesholom is the first Jewish congregation in Indiana and also the second oldest Reform Congregation west of the Allegheny Mountains. By the late 1840s, organized Jewish community life in Indiana began.

The first Jewish organization in the state was the Society for Visiting the Sick and Burying the Dead. It was founded in Fort Wayne in 1848. In 1861, the Society officially adopted the name of Achduth Vesholom Congregation. In 1859, a former church at Wayne and Harrison Streets was dedicated as the first synagogue. The congregation began as Orthodox but by 1874 it had joined the present-day Union for Reform Judaism.

The first purpose-built synagogue was dedicated in 1867, adjacent to the old one. In 1917, a new larger synagogue was dedicated at Wayne and Fairfield. This Classical Revival building remained in use until the present Mid-Century Modern facility on Old Mill Road was dedicated in 1961. A Holocaust Memorial in the form of a wall and a Biblical Garden are in the front of the building. The sanctuary has stained glass windows, many of which are from the Fairfield and Wayne building. In 2012, the temple became part of the Rifkin Campus at 5200 which now houses the temple, local Jewish Federation, Jewish Cemetery Association and Brightpoint Head Start. The 3,000-square-foot Madge Rothschild Resource Center began in 2015 and houses a library and museum promoting Indiana Jewish history and Holocaust education.

Congregation Achduth VeSholom maintains a section at Lindenwood Cemetery on West Main Street. An earlier burial ground located at what is now McCulloch Park was established in 1848. This area became unsuitable for a cemetery due to encroaching development. In 1884, land was purchased at Lindenwood Cemetery and all burials from the old cemetery were relocated to the new cemetery by 1904.

IOWA

Temple Emanuel

It is believed that the first permanent Jewish settler in Iowa was Alexander Levi who came to Dubuque in 1833 from New Orleans and opened a grocery store. Others came starting in the late 1830s or early 1840s. The first Jewish community in Iowa was organized in 1855 at Keokuk, but that community is no longer in existence.

The oldest existing Jewish congregation is in Davenport and was formed as Congregation B'nai Israel in 1861 and incorporated in 1868. At first the congregation included both Orthodox and Reform elements in the services and organization of the congregation. The first step to determine the direction of the congregation was joining what is now the Union of Reform Judaism in 1879. In 1885, the first synagogue was built on Ripley Street between Fourth & Fifth Streets. The building, designed with both Moorish and Romanesque details, was known as Temple Emanuel in honor of Moses Emanuel Rothschild. The second location was at Brady and Eleventh Streets. Dedicated in 1906, it was in a style reminiscent of English country architecture.

In 1943, the congregation decided to build a new structure as soon as the war was over. A site at the corner of Twelfth Street and Mississippi Avenue was purchased in 1944 and ground was broken in 1951. This new structure was designed by synagogue architect Percival Goodman. Dedication of the first building in the Davenport religious community to use modern architecture took place in 1953.

Temple Emanuel owns Mount Nebo Cemetery, which was founded 1851 and is accessed through the Pine Hill Cemetery.

Above: Davenport, Iowa: Temple Emanuel—Exterior of the Brady Street temple, n.d.; Courtesy of the Author's Collection.

Below: Davenport, Iowa: Temple Emanuel—Vintage postcard image of present temple exterior, ca. 1960's; Courtesy of the Author's Collection

KANSAS

Ohev Sholom, Prairie Village & Emanu-El, Wichita

The first Jewish congregation in Kansas, B'nai Jeshurun, was established in Leavenworth in 1859. The Leavenworth congregation, however, no longer exists, but their synagogue built in 1866 at 6th and Osage still stands and has served as apartments since the 1970s when the congregation dissolved. Congregation Emanu-El in Wichita and Ohev Sholom in Prairie Village are both featured because each has unique and historic ties to organized Jewish life in the state.

Wichita's Congregation Emanu-El was formed in 1885 and met in rented facilities before its first purpose-built synagogue was dedicated in 1932. The Art Deco building at East Second and North Fountain Streets contained a Sanctuary, classrooms, offices and a library. That building is now used as the Wichita Community Theater. As the congregation expanded a new synagogue was built at 7011 East Central. Dedicated in 1961, the complex contains a circular tent-like flat-roofed sanctuary, a domed community hall and a classroom and office wing. A large menorah, similar to that at the Israeli Knesset, stands on the grounds in front of the synagogue. Congregation Emanu-El is a member of the Union for Reform Judaism. The congregation maintains the Temple Emanu-El Cemetery which was established in the 1870s and is a section of the Highland Park Cemetery at Hillside and 9th Streets.

Ohev Sholom Congregation in Prairie Village, Kansas, traces its beginnings to 1877. Its forerunners were an Orthodox burial society and two congregations, Gomel Chesed and She'erith Israel. Chevre Bikur Cholim, the Orthodox burial society, was begun in 1877 and incorporated in Kansas City, Missouri, in 1879. In 1887 Congregation Gomel Chesed was incorporated in Kansas City, Missouri, and in 1893 they built their first synagogue at 925 State Line just 20 feet from the Kansas state line. In 1903, the synagogue was destroyed by a flood and the following year they incorporated in Kansas and purchased a building in Kansas City. The She'erith Israel Congregation in Kansas City was also chartered in 1904 and that year they purchased a former church in the city. The two congregations merged together successfully in 1922 and named the new, unified entity, Ohev Sholom. They dedicated their new Classical Revival style synagogue in 1925 at 7th & Sandusky in Kansas City the first purpose-built synagogue in the state. It was demolished in 1964.

By the 1950s much of the membership had moved from Kansas City, Kansas proper to Johnson County, Kansas, and a new synagogue was needed. Land was purchased in 1955 and in 1962 phase one was dedicated at 75th and Nall in Prairie Village, Kansas. In 1970, the congregation dedicated phase two, including a modern tent-shaped sanctuary. Ohev Sholom has owned synagogue property in Kansas longer than any other Jewish congregation. It is a member of the United Synagogue of Conservative Judaism.

Wichita, Kansas: Congregation Emanu-El—Exterior of the present temple, 2008; Courtesy of David Broddle.

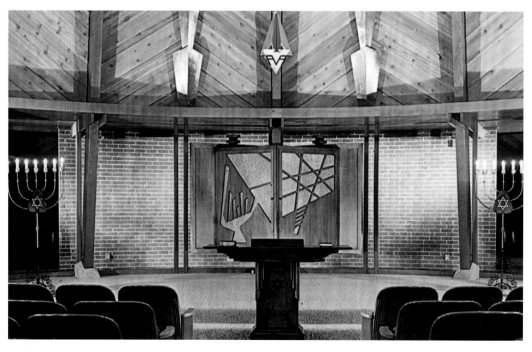

Wichita, Kansas: Congregation Emanu-El—Vintage postcard of the sanctuary interior of the present temple; 1960's; Courtesy of the Author's Collection.

Wichita, Kansas: Congregation Emanu-El—Sketch of the former Fountain Street temple, n.d.; Courtesy of theAuthor's Collection.

Kansas City, Kansas: Congregation Ohev Sholom—Exterior of the 7th and Sandusky Streets synagogue, ca. 1960; Courtesy of Congregation Ohev Sholom, Photographer: Marvin Denton.

Prairie Village, Kansas: Congregation Ohev Sholom—Exterior of the present synagogue, 2016; Courtesy of Congregation Ohev Sholom and Jennifer Schwartz.

Prairie Village, Kansas: Congregation Ohev Sholom—Sanctuary interior of the present synagogue, 2016; Courtesy of Congregation Ohev Sholom and Jennifer Schwartz.

KENTUCKY

The Temple-Congregation Adath Israel Brith Sholom

Jewish merchants with names such as Gratz, Franks and Levy from Philadelphia and Lancaster, Pennsylvania, were heavily involved in commercial and land ventures in areas that would become the states of Kentucky, Tennessee, Indiana, Ohio and Illinois. The first Jewish settler, however, is believed to be John I. Jacob, who settled in Shepherdsville in 1802 and later moved to Louisville.

The first Jewish religious service in Kentucky took place in Louisville in 1838. It was here that the first congregation, Adath Israel, was founded in 1842 and chartered in 1843. The congregation followed the Reform ritual. As the Jewish community grew, another Reform congregation, Brith Sholom, was founded in 1880. The close association of these two congregations ultimately resulted in their merger in 1976. At the time Adath Israel was worshiping in its Classical Revival style temple located at 834 S. 3rd Street, which was dedicated in 1906. Brith Sholom was worshiping in their Colonial Revival style synagogue at 1649 Cowling Avenue, dedicated in 1951. The first home of the merged congregation was the Cowling Avenue location, in use until a new modern structure on Brownsboro Road and Lime Kiln Lane was dedicated in 1980. The Temple is a fine example of Contemporary synagogue architecture. There is a glass enclosed atrium lobby, main sanctuary, chapel, auditorium, and school and administrative wings. The complex has a series of light towers and bands of faceted glass windows.

The first Jewish cemetery in Kentucky was established by Adath Israel prior to 1859. This cemetery, known as the "Hebrew Cemetery," was located at the SW corner of Preston and Kentucky. It was used until the site was needed for highway construction and all the graves were moved to the present Adath Israel Cemetery on Preston Highway south of Eastern Parkway. This cemetery was established in 1873 and was combined under one administration with the ca. 1887 Brith Sholom Cemetery, also on Preston Highway when the two congregations merged.

Louisville, Kentucky: The Temple-Congregation Adath Israel Brith Sholom—Vintage postcard of Temple Adath Israel on South Third Street, n.d.; Courtesy of Special Collections, College of Charleston Libraries.

Louisville, Kentucky: The Temple-Congregation Adath Israel Brith Sholom—Exterior of the former Cowling Avenue location of Brith Sholom Congregation, ca. 1997; Courtesy of the Author's Collection.

Louisville, Kentucky: The Temple-Congregation Adath Israel Brith Sholom—Sanctuary exterior of the Brownsboro Road temple, ca. 1997; Courtesy of the Author's Collection.

Louisville, Kentucky: The Temple-Congregation Adath Israel Brith Sholom—Main entrance to the Brownsboro Road temple, ca. 1997; Courtesy of the Author's Collection.

LOUISIANA

Touro Synagogue

Jews settled in the French colony at the start of the 18th century despite the Black Code of 1724, which banned Jews from the colony. The code was invalidated in 1803 when the Louisiana Purchase became United States territory.

The first Jewish congregation in the state, Shangarai Chesed or Gates of Mercy, was formed and incorporated in New Orleans in 1828. One of the founders was Judah Touro, an early Jewish settler in New Orleans and noted philanthropist. The congregation was composed of German-Jewish and Portuguese-Jewish settlers, but followed the German rite of worship. In 1846, a second congregation, Nefuzoth Yehudah or Dispersed of Judah, was founded by those preferring the Spanish-Portuguese ritual. Dispersed of Judah Congregation was incorporated in 1847. The two groups existed independently until 1881 when they merged to become Congregation Shangarai Chessed Nefuzoth Yehudah. Touro's financial generosity was instrumental to both congregations and it was decided to name the new congregation to honor him. Known as the *Touro Synagogue* after the merger, the name was not legally changed until 1937.

The congregation joined the Reform movement in 1891. Today it is the oldest Jewish congregation beyond the coastal colonial cities. The current and fifth location was built in 1908 and designed by Emil Weil. It is an impressive Byzantine style structure that has a massive dome and beautiful stained glass windows. The columns that support the ark were presented by Judah Touro in 1854 and have been moved from each location and are now in the current sanctuary. The synagogue complex contains the Norman Synagogue House, assembly hall, pavilion and Bowsky Gardens, all of which were completed in 1989. Touro Synagogue is located along St. Charles Avenue near the famous Garden District.

The congregation's first cemetery was established in 1828 at 2000 Jackson Avenue near Benton and Saratoga Streets and was in use until about 1868. In 1859, the congregation purchased land at 4100 Frenchman Street for the Hebrew Rest Cemetery No. 1. The need for more space led to the purchase of additional land across the street at 4101 Frenchman Street. This burial lot was enlarged in 1938. The Dispersed of Judah Cemetery is on Canal Street between South Anthony and Helena Streets on land donated by Judah Touro in 1850.

New Orleans, Louisiana: Touro Synagogue—Vintage postcard of the Touro Synagogue, 1913; Courtesy of Special Collections, College of Charleston Libraries.

MAINE

Congregation Beth Israel

Jews were involved in the lumber trade in Bangor and constituted a fairly large Jewish community by the late 1840's. The first congregation in the state was Ahabat Achim which was formed about 1840 and chartered in 1849. As the Jewish population left because of dwindling timber reserves, the congregation disbanded after almost twenty years of existence.

The present Jewish community in Maine dates from the mid-1880s when an informal religious association was formed in Bangor. That group became Beth Israel and was formally organized in 1888. It is the oldest permanent Jewish congregation in Maine. It was the first congregation to erect a synagogue dedicated in 1907. The wooden building was located on Center Street and contained a sanctuary, a women's gallery and basement. Disaster struck in 1911 when fire destroyed nearly 400 buildings including Beth Israel. The congregation immediately began planning for a new building and purchased land on York Street overlooking the Penobscot River. The new synagogue was dedicated in 1912 and was designed by Henry Lewen, an expert in fireproof construction. The exterior features Classical detailing and a multi-sided dome. The congregation continues to worship in the structure today. Though Orthodox at its founding, Congregation Beth Israel moved toward the Conservative form of ritual and in 1948 affiliated with the Conservative movement.

The Beth Israel Cemetery is at Mount Hope Avenue in Bangor and dates to 1884. The 1840 cemetery that belonged to the defunct Ahabat Achim still exists on Webster Avenue.

Bangor, Maine: Congregation Beth Israel—Exterior of the present synagogue, ca. 2015; Courtesy of Waymarking.com User: BK-Hunters

MARYLAND

Baltimore Hebrew Congregational

Jews have lived in Maryland since before the American Revolution, but due to a lack of religious freedom, their numbers were small. The passage of the "The Jew Bill" in 1826 enabled Jews to hold public office and permitted some measure of religious freedom. The first Jewish organization and congregation in Maryland was chartered in 1830 in Baltimore. The Baltimore Hebrew Congregation, founded as Nidche Yisrael or The Scattered of Israel, began as German Orthodox but later changed to Reform. The first synagogue in the state was dedicated in 1845 on Lloyd Street in East Baltimore. The Greek Revival structure is now part of the Jewish Museum of Maryland. It is the third oldest extant synagogue building in the country and a national and local historic landmark.

As the congregation prospered, many members began moving out of downtown to fashionable neighborhoods in the northwest portions of the city. In 1891, the congregation dedicated a magnificent synagogue on Madison Avenue at Robert Street. The Madison Avenue Temple is an excellent example of Byzantine Revival architecture. It is now a church and a registered landmark. The Jewish population continued their move to the northwest and in 1951 the new Park Heights Avenue Temple was dedicated. Designed by synagogue architect Percival Goodman, it is located at the corner of Park Heights Avenue and Charlesworth Road in the Upper Park Heights neighborhood of Baltimore.

The complex contains a sanctuary noted for its art murals, an elliptical chapel (1967), an auditorium, art gallery, classrooms, offices and a library. The sanctuary facade contains large bas-relief sculptures by George Aarons.

Baltimore Hebrew Congregation maintains two cemeteries. The first, established in 1832, is at 2100 Belaire Road. The second and current cemetery at 400 Berryman's Lane in suburban Reisterstown was dedicated in1965. A cemetery of historic note to Maryland Jewry is the Etting Family Burial Ground at West North Avenue and Pennsylvania Avenue in Baltimore. Established in 1799, it is the oldest Jewish cemetery in Baltimore and contains 25 graves of early prominent Maryland Jews. Also of interest is the former "Cohen Family Burial Ground," founded in 1834 on Saratoga Street near Carey Street. Forty-four members of the Cohen family were buried there and in 1974 a court approved relocation of the graves took place. They now rest in the "Cohen Section" of the Baltimore Hebrew Cemetery on Belair Road.

Baltimore, Maryland: Baltimore Hebrew Congregation—Vintage postcard of the exterior of the present temple, 1960's; Courtesy of the Author's Collection.

Baltimore, Maryland: Baltimore Hebrew Congregation—Front entrance facade of the present temple, 1995; Courtesy of the Author's Collection.

Above left: Baltimore, Maryland: Baltimore Hebrew Congregation—Exterior of the former Madison Avenue temple, 2011; Courtesy of Wikimedia Commons User: Acroterion.

Above right: Baltimore, Maryland: Baltimore Hebrew Congregation—Exterior of the Lloyd Street Synagogue, 2011; Courtesy of Wikimedia Commons User: KudzuVine.

Below: Baltimore, Maryland: Baltimore Hebrew Congregation—Sanctuary interior of the Lloyd Street Synagogue, 1958; Courtesy of the Library of Congress Prints & Photographs Division, HABS, MD,4-BALT,117–3. Photograph: Lanny Miyamoto.

MASSACHUSETTS

Congregation Ohabei Shalom

Massachusetts' first congregation, Ohabei Shalom or Lovers of Peace, was founded in 1842 in Boston. A cemetery in East Boston was established in 1844 and the congregation was chartered the following year. By 1851, the first synagogue building in the state was built on Warrenton Street. Located in Boston's South End, the two-story wooden synagogue was consecrated in 1852. It is thought that the Touro Synagogue in Newport served as the model. In 1863, a former church was purchased across from the previous temple. This structure is now the home of the Charles Playhouse.

As growth continued, the congregation moved into their third synagogue, a former church, located on Union Park Street in the South End. The land for the present synagogue was purchased in 1921. The Temple Center building, which houses a 400-seat chapel, was constructed in 1925. The beautiful Byzantine-Romanesque Revival domed sanctuary was completed in 1928 and is a familiar landmark on Beacon Street in Brookline. A modern Education Center was built in 2009 adjacent to the temple.

Began as an Orthodox congregation following the Polish ritual, Ohabei Shalom instituted a number of reforms beginning in 1870, and in 1871 voted to become a Reform congregation. In 1881, they joined the present-day Union for Reform Judaism. Ohabei Shalom is the oldest Reform congregation in New England.

The congregation maintains the first Jewish cemetery in Massachusetts, begun in 1844 on Wordsworth Street near Byron and Homer Streets. Prior to this date, Jewish burials had to take place outside of Massachusetts. The newest cemetery used by Ohabei Shalom is a section of Sharon Memorial Park. Located on Dedham Street in Sharon, Massachusetts, it is known as the Ahava Section Ohabei Shalom of Brookline.

Brookline, Massachusetts: Temple Ohabei Shalom—Exterior of the present temple, n.d.; Courtesy of Samuel D. Gruber.

MICHIGAN

Temple Beth El

Michigan's first Jewish religious services were held in Ann Arbor in 1845, and in 1849, the first Jewish burial ground in the state was established. By 1850, many Ann Arbor Jews had moved to Detroit, which was becoming the commercial capital of Michigan. Michigan's first Jewish congregation was established in 1850 in Detroit as the Orthodox Beth El Society. 1856 witnessed many changes towards reform, and in 1873 Temple Beth El became a charter member of what is now the Union for Reform Judaism.

Beth El's first permanent location was a former church purchased in 1861 on Rivard Street. Another former church was purchased on Washington Boulevard and Clifford Street in 1867 to serve a growing congregation. As the congregation grew, a new grand synagogue was built on Woodward Avenue and Eliot in 1903. This Beaux-Arts domed synagogue was designed by the noted Detroit architect, Albert Kahn. The building now serves as the Wayne State University Bonstelle Theater. By 1922, the membership had exceeded 800 families and a new temple was built at Woodward Avenue and Gladstone. The congregation again employed Albert Kahn, who designed a Greek Revival style temple. The Jewish Community continued the move north and into the suburbs and this trend continued into the 1960s.

In 1973, Temple Beth El dedicated its current facilities on Telegraph Road in suburban Bloomfield Hills. The ultra-modern sanctuary was designed by the renowned architect Minoru Yamasaki. There is also a chapel, library, archives, museum, and classroom and office space. The tent-like sanctuary is a well-recognized landmark. Beth El was one of the last synagogues to relocate out of the city.

Temple Beth El has three cemeteries in the Detroit area. The oldest, a historic landmark, is located on Lafayette Boulevard east of downtown Detroit and was established in 1851 as the Chaplain Street Cemetery of Temple Beth El. Woodmere Cemetery Section North F also serves Temple Beth El and was established in 1873. The newest cemetery is in suburban Livonia. Beth El Memorial Park on 6 Mile Road was established in 1940.

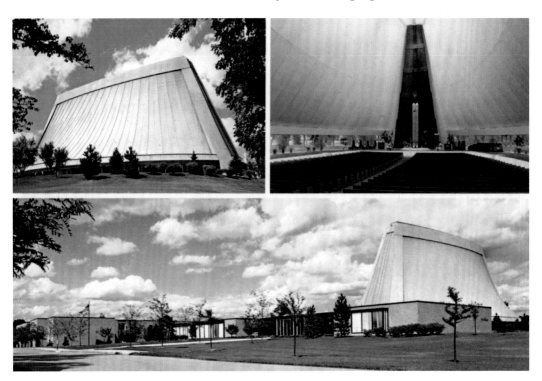

Bloomfield Hills, Michigan: Temple Beth El—Vintage postcard featuring the present sanctuary exterior and interior, 1960's; Courtesy of Special Collections, College of Charleston Libraries.

Bloomfield Hills, Michigan: Temple Beth El—Entrance and front facade of the present temple, 1995; Courtesy of the Author's Collection.

Above: Detroit, Michigan: Temple Beth El—Exterior of the former Woodward Avenue & Eliot temple, n.d.; Courtesy of the Library of Congress Prints & Photographs Division, LC-DIG-det-4a17986.

Below: Detroit, Michigan: Temple Beth El—Sanctuary interior of the former Woodward Avenue & Eliot temple, n.d.; Courtesy of Temple Beth El Buildings Collection, Rabbi Leo. M. Franklin Archives, Temple Beth El, Bloomfield Hills, Michigan.

Above: Detroit, Michigan: Temple Beth El—Exterior of the former Woodward Avenue & Gladstone temple, 1995; Courtesy of the Author's Collection.

Below: Detroit, Michigan: Temple Beth El—Sanctuary interior of the former Woodward Avenue & Gladstone temple, n.d.; Courtesy of Temple Beth El Buildings Collection, Rabbi Leo. M. Franklin Archives, Temple Beth El, Bloomfield Hills, Michigan.

MINNESOTA

Mount Zion Temple

It is believed that Jews first came to Minnesota around the year 1849. Mount Zion Temple was organized as the Mount Zion Hebrew Association in 1856, just two years after the city of St. Paul was incorporated. In 1857, the Mount Zion Hebrew Association received a charter from the territory and in 1862 the association became a congregation.

Their first synagogue at Tenth and Minnesota Streets was built in 1871. The wooden structure with Gothic details served the congregation until 1882 when a new Byzantine Revival style brick synagogue was dedicated on the same site. During this period, the congregation adopted many reforms in worship and in 1878 became a member of the Reform movement.

As the members moved from away from the lower part of town the leaders of the congregation agreed upon another move for Mount Zion. The third synagogue was located in a fashionable area at the corner of Holly and Avon. Dedicated in 1904, the new domed synagogue was designed with both Greek and Byzantine styling. A new assembly hall was built in 1927 to accommodate the expanded activities.

In the fall of 1945, a site at Summit Avenue between Hamline and Syndicate was purchased, and in 1954 the fourth synagogue, designed by the noted German Jewish architect Erich Mendelsohn, was dedicated. The building was a complete departure from the traditional styles previously used. It was completely modern with its smooth surfaces and attention to symbolism in design rather than added details. The main features are the rectangular towers of the main sanctuary and the chapel which project upward from the centers of these areas in the base of the building. The structure is a prominent landmark.

The first Jewish burial ground in Minnesota was on Jackson Street and Front and served until 1889 when transfers were made to the new cemetery at Payne and Larpenteur. For a long time, the original Mount Zion Cemetery was the only Jewish burial ground in Minnesota. Many of the early burials from the original cemetery were residents from towns in Iowa and North Dakota.

Saint Paul, Minnesota: Mount Zion Temple— Exterior of the Tenth & Minnesota Streets temple, n.d.; Courtesy of Mount Zion Temple.

Above: Saint Paul, Minnesota: Mount Zion Temple—Exterior of the new 1882 temple at Tenth & Minnesota Streets, n.d.; Courtesy of Mount Zion Temple.

Below: Saint Paul, Minnesota: Mount Zion Temple—Exterior of the Holly Avenue & Avon Street temple, n.d.; Courtesy of Mount Zion Temple.

Above: Saint Paul, Minnesota: Mount Zion Temple—Exterior of the present Summit Avenue temple, n.d.; Courtesy of Mount Zion Temple.

Below: Saint Paul, Minnesota: Mount Zion Temple—Sanctuary interior of the present Summit Avenue temple, n.d.; Courtesy of Mount Zion Temple.

MISSISSIPPI

Temple B'nai Israel's

Natchez is the home of the oldest Jewish congregation in the State of Mississippi and one of the oldest in the South. Temple B'nai Israel traces its beginnings to the Jewish cemetery established in 1840 and the resulting burial society formally organized in 1843. The Natchez Jewish community of the 19th century was primarily of German and Alsatian origin and once established became the merchant class in town.

At first, worship and other activities were conducted in members' homes and in rented quarters. With the onset of the Civil War, all activities came to a standstill. The community reorganized after the war and dedicated its first temple in 1872 at Washington and Commerce Streets. Also in 1872, the congregation changed its name to B'nai Israel, received a charter, and began to adopt many reforms in the service. B'nai Israel joined the Reform movement in 1874. The congregation worshiped in the Washington Street temple until it was destroyed by fire in November of 1903.

The present temple was dedicated on the same site in 1905. This magnificent domed Classical Revival synagogue is located in a National historic district. Natchez, as well as other small Southern towns, experienced declines in their Jewish populations as the younger generation sought the increased social, business and religious opportunities in the larger Jewish communities in the South and elsewhere. Because of this decline, B'nai Israel deeded their building to the Museum of the Southern Experience of the Institute for the Southern Jewish Experience in 1991. The museum uses the building as an adjunct museum, but Jewish religious services will be held in the building until such time as the congregation disbands.

Congregation B'nai Israel maintains three sections of the City Cemetery, with the earliest portion dating to 1840.

Above: Natchez, Mississippi: Temple B'nai Israel—Exterior of the present temple, 2006; Courtesy of the Library of Congress Prints & Photographs Division, HABS, MS-276-2.

Below: Natchez, Mississippi: Temple B'nai Israel—Sanctuary interior of the present temple, 2006; Courtesy of the Library of Congress Prints & Photographs Division, HABS, MS-276-3.

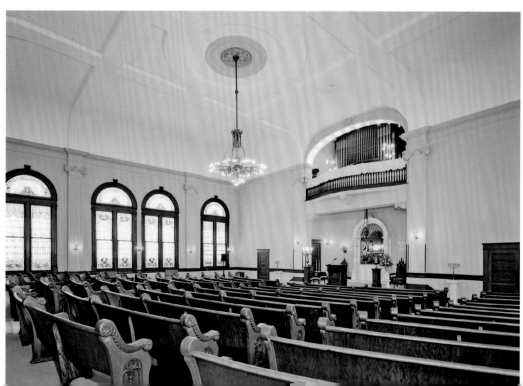

MISSOURI

United Hebrew Congregation

St. Louis is the home of the oldest Jewish congregation in the state and the oldest west of the Mississippi River. It was formed in 1837 when the first Jewish worship service west of the Mississippi took place. By 1841 the worship group was formally organized as the United Hebrew Congregation. In 1848, a former church on Fifth Street near Green was purchased for a synagogue. In 1859 a new synagogue, at Sixth Street between Locust and St. Charles, was dedicated. United Hebrew began as an Orthodox congregation and embraced reforms slowly. In 1878, the congregation affiliated with the Reform movement, withdrew in 1885 and rejoined in 1904.

The congregation followed the movement of the Jewish community westward in the city and in 1879 relocated to Olive and Twenty-First Streets. Another move in 1903 took the congregation to a former church at Kingshighway and Enright. In 1927, the United Hebrew Congregation dedicated its magnificent synagogue at 225 South Skinker Boulevard in the University City area. The domed synagogue, designed in the Byzantine Revival style, contains a 40-foot-high sanctuary with plaster reliefs, leaded amber glass windows and alabaster and bronze chandeliers. At the time, it was said to be the third largest synagogue in the country. It now houses the Missouri Historical Society.

The Jewish population continued the move westward and in 1977, United Hebrew Congregation built the Gudder Educational Center on Conway and Woods Mill Roads in suburban Chesterfield as a west campus for the Religious and Hebrew School. In the late 1980s, construction began on a sanctuary and large chapel that were dedicated in 1989. The architect was Pietro Belluschi, a noted modern architect who designed synagogues in Pennsylvania, New York and Massachusetts. The hallmark of the sanctuary is the glass dome that serves as a skylight and appears as a beautiful kippah, or skullcap.

United Hebrew Congregation's cemetery is at 7855 Canton in University City. It was purchased in 1866 and was known as the Mount Olive Cemetery until 1960 when the name was changed to United Hebrew Cemetery. An earlier cemetery from 1840 is thought to have been located at 2700 Pratte Avenue.

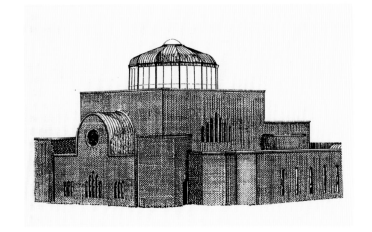

Saint Louis, Missouri: United Hebrew Congregation—Sketch of the sanctuary portion of the present temple, n.d.; Courtesy of the Author's Collection.

Saint Louis, Missouri: United Hebrew Congregation – Exterior of the former Skinker Boulevard temple, 1928; Courtesy of the Author's Collection (*The American Architect* November 5, 1928)

Saint Louis, Missouri: United Hebrew Congregation – Sanctuary interior of the former Skinker Boulevard temple, 1928; Courtesy of the Author's Collection (*The American Architect* November 5, 1928).

MONTANA

Temple B'nai Israel

The first permanent Jewish settlement in Montana was in the town of Helena where the Hebrew Benevolent Society, established in 1866, became the nucleus for Congregation Emanuel. The congregation disbanded in 1964. Their Moorish Revival style synagogue from 1891 is now offices for the local Catholic Diocese.

The oldest existing Jewish congregation is B'nai Israel Congregation in Butte. It was formally organized in 1897 with origins in the Hebrew Benevolent Association established in 1881. B'nai Israel began with a Reform orientation, as most of the organizers were of German origin. At one time, the Butte Jewish community supported three synagogues, one Reform and two Orthodox.

B'nai Israel constructed its first and only synagogue in 1903 at Washington and Galena Streets in the city's Uptown section. The red-brick synagogue with onion-domed tower used exotic architectural influences typical in synagogues of the period. Brick and stone were mandated building materials after a devastating fire in 1879 in Butte. The B'nai Israel synagogue is the oldest such building in continuous use in Montana.

The Jewish community declined in numbers as the overall economy of the city fell beginning in the 1960s. The three congregations in the city then decided to merge into one congregation around 1968.

B'nai Israel's cemetery is next to the Mount Moriah Cemetery. It was established by the Hebrew Benevolent Society in 1881 and deeded to B'nai Israel in 1905.

Above: Butte, Montana: Congregation B'nai Israel—Notecard sketch of the exterior of the present temple, 1976; Courtesy of the Author's Collection. Original Watercolor: Sonia Berman Ehrlich.

Left: Butte, Montana: Congregation B'nai Israel—Sanctuary interior of the present temple, 2016; Courtesy of Congregation B'nai Israel.

NEBRASKA

Temple Israel

Jews began settling in Nebraska in the 1850s and High Holy Days services in Omaha were held during the 1860s. Congregation of Israel, today's Temple Israel, was founded in Omaha in 1871 and incorporated in 1873. Temple Israel dedicated the first synagogue building in Nebraska in 1884 at 23rd and Harney. It was a frame structure with a stained glass window, Hebrew lettering and a Star of David on the front facade.

Reforms began to be introduced and in 1889 the congregation joined the Reform movement and took the new name of Temple Israel. A new synagogue at Park Avenue and Jackson Street was dedicated in 1908. It was a domed structure that included Classical, Byzantine and French influences. In 1926, a religious school was built.

The Jewish community shifted westward by the 1940s and the need for a new and larger temple arose. A new modern temple at 7023 Cass Street was dedicated in 1954. The Park Avenue Temple was sold to the St. John's Greek Orthodox Church, which still occupies the building today. The Cass Street temple featured a sanctuary, chapel, social hall, classrooms and offices. Further movement of the Jewish population westward necessitated another move and in 2013 a Post-Modern temple was dedicated at 132nd and Pacific in Sterling Ridge. The chapel Ark and sanctuary stained glass windows from the Cass Street temple were moved to the new location.

Temple Israel's cemetery established in 1871 and is at 6412 North 42nd Street. The cemetery, originally known as the Pleasant Hill Cemetery, was purchased by the original B'nai Israel Society which disbanded and deeded the property to Temple Israel.

Omaha, Nebraska: Temple Israel—Exterior of the present temple, 2016; Courtesy of Temple Israel.

Omaha, Nebraska: Temple Israel—Exterior of the present temple, 2016; Courtesy of Temple Israel.

Omaha, Nebraska: Temple Israel—Sanctuary interior of the present temple, 2016; Courtesy of Temple Israel.

Omaha, Nebraska: Temple Israel—Exterior of the former Cass Street temple, 2008; Courtesy of the Author's Collection.

Omaha, Nebraska: Temple Israel—Vintage postcard of the former Park Avenue temple, n.d.; Courtesy of Author's Collection.

NEVADA

Temple Emanu-El

Jews and thousands of others found Nevada a popular place to settle because of the desire to strike it rich in the gold and silver mines. By 1864, a Jewish congregation was organized in Virginia City where most of the Jewish settlers lived. The Jewish community of Virginia City soon faded and disappeared as the mines became a thing of the past.

The oldest existing congregation today is in Reno. Temple Emanu-El traces its origins to the Hebrew Benevolent Society established in 1879, and the Young Men's Hebrew Association founded in 1908. The purpose of the YMHA organization was to arrange for the building of a temple. It was not until 1917, however, that the Temple Emanu-El Association was formed. Land was purchased at 426 West Street for the new synagogue. Building plans were shelved due to the onset of World War One. Despite the setbacks in the attempt to build Reno's first Jewish house of worship, ground was broken in 1921 with a dedication in 1922. The brick synagogue had two towers, a central round stained glass window on the upper facade and stained glass windows on the side walls.

By the early 1970s the membership had increased substantially and a larger and more convenient synagogue was needed. The downtown synagogue was sold and land was purchased on the corner of Manzanita Lane and Lakeside. Groundbreaking took place in 1972 and the new synagogue was dedicated in 1973. Additions of classrooms, offices and a chapel were completed in 1981.

The synagogue is Contemporary in design with a sanctuary that sweeps upward in a curved fashion. The upper part of the sanctuary wall opposite the bimah contains stained glass strip-windows. The Emanuel Berger Library building contains stained glass windows saved from the West Street synagogue.

The cemetery for the congregation, the Reno Hebrew Cemetery, is on Angel Street a half mile from the casino/hotel district. It was established in 1876 and chartered in 1878. It is operated and administered jointly by Temple Emanu-El and the Reform Temple Sinai.

Reno, Nevada: Temple Emanu-El: Exterior of the present synagogue, ca. 2008; Courtesy of the Author's Collection.

NEW HAMPSHIRE

Temple Adath Yeshurun

It was not until the latter part of the 19th century that Jewish communities began to take root in New Hampshire. The oldest existing congregation, Adath Yeshurun, is found in Manchester.

Congregation Adath Yeshurun traces its beginnings to the B'nai Jeshurun Congregation established in 1889. Adath Yeshurun was formed about two years later in 1891 as the successor to B'nai Jeshurun, and was incorporated in 1900. In 1911, the first synagogue in Manchester was dedicated on Central Street. The first structure built for a Manchester Jewish congregation was a frame building and had an upstairs sanctuary with balcony, a kitchen and a downstairs social hall. A major renovation took place in the 1930s.

Adath Yeshurun began as an Orthodox congregation and remained a traditional one until the mid-1950s when the congregation became Reform. As the congregation began to grow, the need for a larger and more convenient building became evident. The change to Reform also helped to galvanize the need for a new synagogue. A site located on Prospect Street near the Jewish Community Center was purchased and the noted synagogue architect, Percival Goodman, was engaged to design the new building completed in 1959. The building is typical of Goodman's designs with the extensive use of brick and wood. The sanctuary has a pitched roof and a large sculptural panel on the front facade. The building contains a social hall, library, classrooms and offices. A Holocaust Memorial, created by Manchester artist Armand Szainer, is located on the grounds.

Adath Yeshurun's cemetery is on South Beech Street and was purchased in 1896. It replaced an earlier burial ground on South River Road in Bedford in which only a few bodies had been interred. In 1918 Congregation Anshe Sfard purchased land for its cemetery next to that of Adath Yeshurun. In the late 1930s, the two cemeteries were combined into one cemetery.

Above: Manchester, New Hampshire: Temple Adath Yeshurun—Exterior of the present temple, ca. 2008; Courtesy of the Author's Collection.

Below: Manchester, New Hampshire: Temple Adath Yeshurun—Interior of the present temple sanctuary, ca. 2008; Courtesy of the Author's Collection.

NEW JERSEY

Congregation B'nai Jeshurun—Nathan Barnert Memorial Temple

Jews have lived in New Jersey since the 18th century, but permanent Jewish communities did not develop until the 1840s. The first and oldest Jewish congregation in the state was established in 1847 in Paterson. Organized as the Congregation B'nai Jeshurun of the Town of Paterson, it was incorporated shorty after formation.

The first permanent synagogue was acquired in 1882 at 124 Van Houten Street. In 1894, their first purpose-built temple was dedicated at Broadway and Straight Street. This Moorish Revival twin towered structure was built with funds donated by Mr. Nathan Barnert and his wife Miriam. Barnert, an immigrant from Germany, was a successful businessman, philanthropist, and mayor of Paterson. The new temple was named in his honor.

Began as an Orthodox congregation, a gradual shift towards Reform began to take place in the 1870s. Though there is no official record of the congregation's adoption of Reform Judaism, by 1920 B'nai Jeshurun had formalized its ties with Reform movement. The congregation grew and members began relocating out of the older neighborhoods after World War Two.

B'nai Jeshurun built a new synagogue designed by Percival Goodman in a fashionable residential area of the city. The structure at Derrom Avenue and Broadway was Contemporary in design and dedicated in 1965. It now houses a mosque. Further movement continued out of the city limits, and in 1987 a new synagogue was dedicated in suburban Franklin Lakes. This structure was also designed by Percival Goodman and was one of his last projects. The design includes a pitched roof, a dormer style ark tower, and stained glass windows. The use of natural elements in the exterior is typical of many of Goodman's synagogues.

The original cemetery is in what was Centerville in Acquackanonck Township and now the Richfield section of Clifton. This congregation had all visible tombstones removed to the current cemetery site and the former cemetery site today is in the middle of a residential neighborhood. The current cemetery is Mount Nebo, established in 1866 and on Totowa Avenue in Totowa, New Jersey.

Franklin Lakes, New Jersey: The Barnert Temple-Congregation B'nai Jeshurun—Exterior of the present temple, 2016; Courtesy of Richard Edelman and Congregation B'nai Jeshurun.

Franklin Lakes, New Jersey: The Barnert Temple-Congregation B'nai Jeshurun—Sanctuary interior of the present temple, 2016; Courtesy of Richard Edelman and The Barnert Temple-Congregation B'nai Jeshurun.

Above left: Paterson, New Jersey: The Barnert Temple-Congregation B'nai Jeshurun—Exterior of the former Derrom Avenue temple, 1964; Courtesy of The Barnert Temple-Congregation B'nai Jeshurun.

Above right: Paterson, New Jersey: The Barnert Temple-Congregation B'nai Jeshurun—Vintage postcard of the Broadway temple, n.d.; Courtesy of the Jewish Historical Society of North Jersey.

Below: Paterson, New Jersey: The Barnert Temple-Congregation B'nai Jeshurun—Sanctuary interior of the Broadway temple, n.d.; Courtesy of The Barnert Temple-Congregation B'nai Jeshurun.

NEW MEXICO

Congregation Albert

Some of the earliest known Jews in New Mexico were the Secret Jews or Marranos. Solomon Jacob Spiegelberg was the first practicing Jew to settle in modern day New Mexico and became one of the most well-known businessmen in Santa Fe and the Territory. The first Jewish religious services were held in Santa Fe in 1860.

The first congregation, Montefiore, was established in the town of Las Vegas in 1884. Congregation Montefiore built the first synagogue in New Mexico in 1886. The congregation disbanded around 1950, but the building still stands as the Catholic Newman Center. The oldest existing congregation in the state is found in Albuquerque. Though a considerable number of Jews resided in the city and had organized a B'nai B'rith Lodge (1882), purchased a cemetery and held religious services, a congregation was not established until 1897. The congregation was named Congregation Albert in honor of one of its founders Albert Grunsfeld.

In October 1898, land was purchased at Seventh and Gold for the site of the congregation's first synagogue, which was dedicated in 1900. The structure was a square brick building with rose windows and a large dome. The dome was topped with a small parapet tower. In 1912, the building was completely remodeled and covered with a stucco facade. This structure served the congregation for over 50 years, but no longer stands.

In 1950, a site for a new synagogue was purchased at Lead Avenue between Oak and Mulberry Avenues. The new synagogue was completed in 1951. Designed in the Mid-Century Modern style, the structure was long and low and blended well into the landscape. The exterior walls were decorated with murals. The congregation soon outgrew the existing facilities and a number of additions were built. The present synagogue was dedicated in 1984 at 3800 Louisiana Boulevard, Northeast and is a functional Contemporary structure. Congregation Albert is a member of the Union for Reform Judaism.

The congregation's cemetery is at 700 Yale Avenue on the grounds of the Fairview Cemetery. The cemetery began in 1902 when it acquired the former B'nai B'rith Cemetery established in 1889.

Albuquerque, New Mexico: Congregation Albert—Exterior of the Seventh Street & Gold Avenue temple, n.d.; Courtesy of the Western States Jewish History Association Image: WS- 0397-3-N.

דרשוני וחיין

Albuquerque, New Mexico: Congregation Albert—Exterior of the present temple, 2016; Courtesy of Wikimedia Commons User: John Phelan.

NEW YORK

Shearith Israel—The Spanish & Portuguese Synagogue

The very first settlement of Jews in North America was founded in September 1654 when Jewish refugees from Recife, Brazil, landed at the Dutch colony of New Amsterdam. These individuals were among many who had been expelled from various Portuguese held lands once the Dutch had been conquered. When the group landed in New Amsterdam, they were arrested by Governor Peter Stuyvesant who did not wish to have Jews settling in the colony. They were held until orders were received from the Dutch West India Company in Amsterdam. Because many of the shareholders of the company were Jewish, the governor was pressured to accept these refugees as long as they would not become a burden to the colony.

The refugees almost immediately formed Congregation Shearith Israel. It is the oldest Jewish congregation in North America. The congregation followed the Orthodox Sephardic ritual as it still does today. From its earliest days, Shearith Israel had both Sephardic and Ashkenazic members.

In 1730, their first synagogue on Mill Street in Lower Manhattan, now South William Street, was built. This was the first synagogue in North America built and dedicated as such. A second synagogue was built on the same site in 1818 to serve the needs of a growing congregation. It was a substantial building built of brick and stone and faced with Roman cement. The congregation relocated again in 1834 to Crosby Street between Broome & Spring Streets and built a larger building. Due to population shifts, in 1860 Shearith Israel moved to 5 West 19th Street. The new synagogue was built in the Palladian style and it was noted in several publications of the time. Because of poor acoustics and building accessibility, and as congregants continued their move uptown, talk about building a more suitable synagogue soon began.

The current synagogue is at 70th Street and Central Park West and is a well-known landmark synagogue. It was built in 1897 in the Classical Revival style. The architect was Arnold Brunner, an American-born Jewish architect who was already a distinguished architect. The interior of the synagogue was designed like most Spanish and Portuguese congregations with the reader's desk toward the rear-center of the room. The interior contains marble embellishments and Louis Comfort Tiffany crafted stained glass windows. The chapel, also known as the Little Synagogue, is a replica of the Mill Street synagogue and contains historic furnishings and ritual items from previous synagogue locations.

From 1654 to 1825 Shearith Israel was the only Jewish congregation in New York City and all of the Jews in the city belonged to the congregation. Shearith Israel and its members were involved in important communal enterprises and many local and national Jewish institutions trace their beginnings to members of the congregation.

The congregation maintains a number of cemeteries of historical importance. The first is the Chatham Square cemetery established in 1656, the first Jewish cemetery in North America. It is the second oldest extant Jewish cemetery in North America and is the resting place of many Jewish Revolutionary soldiers and patriots. The second cemetery is on West 11th Street, in the heart of Greenwich Village, and was established in 1805. There is currently a project to restore and beautify the historic burial ground. The third cemetery is on West 21st Street, west of Avenue of the Americas, and was established in 1829. The current cemetery is Shearith Israel Cemetery on Cypress Hills Street in Brooklyn. It is often referred to as the Bet Olam Cemetery and was in use by 1851.

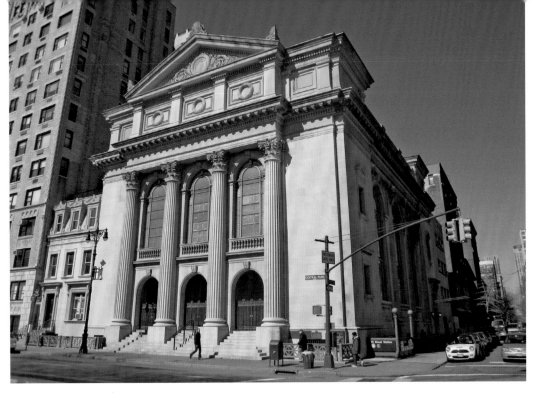

Above: New York City, New York: Congregation Shearith Israel—Exterior of the present Central Park West synagogue, 2012; Courtesy of the Author's Collection.

Below: New York City, New York: Congregation Shearith Israel—Vintage postcard of the present sanctuary interior, n.d.; Courtesy of Special Collections, College of Charleston Libraries.

TEMPLE SHEARITH ISRAEL, HEBREW, 5 WEST 19TH STREET, NEAR FIFTH AVENUE.

New York City, New York: Congregation Shearith Israel—Exterior of the West 19th Street synagogue; Courtesy of Samuel D. Gruber (*King's Handbook of New York*, 1898).

New York City, New York: Congregation Shearith Israel—Interior of the West 19th Street synagogue: Courtesy of Samuel Gruber (*Frank Leslie's Illustrated Newspaper*, September 9, 1860).

NORTH CAROLINA

Temple of Israel

Jews of Spanish & Portuguese origin were among the first Jews to settle in North Carolina during the 18th century. Though North Carolina welcomed Jewish settlers early on, the first organized Jewish community established in Wilmington did not develop until after the Civil War. Many of the early Jewish settlers in town were peddlers of German origin who became merchants. As their roots became permanent, the need for religious services became more pronounced. Religious services were conducted in rented quarters by lay readers, and in 1867, a congregation was formed. The first recorded minutes refer to the name as Mishkan Israel, but it was not until 1873 that the congregation was incorporated as Temple of Israel.

In 1875, the cornerstone of the first synagogue building in North Carolina was dedicated. The elaborate and well attended ceremonies were front page news. The architects were Samuel Sloan and James Walker. The Moorish Revival synagogue was completed in 1876. In 1951, a historical street marker was placed in front of the National Historic Landmark synagogue. It is part of the Wilmington Historic District. The interior of the synagogue features historic artifacts, including a 200-year-old chandelier that hung in the synagogue in Landau in der Pfalz, Germany; French made stained glass windows; a historic Pilcher Tracker Action pipe organ; and a 118-year-old kiddush cup still used during Shabbat services. The pipe organ and interior and exterior have been recently renovated and restored. Temple of Israel is a member of the Union of Reform Judaism and was an early member of the Reform movement. The temple is one of fewer than thirty congregations to endure in its original nineteenth century structure and is the oldest synagogue building in North Carolina.

The cemetery of the congregation is known as the Hebrew Cemetery, as is a separate section of the Oakdale Cemetery. This Jewish section of the cemetery was consecrated in 1856 when the Oakdale cemetery was established and is at 520 North 15th Street.

Wilmington, North Carolina: Temple of Israel—Exterior of the present temple, 2016; Courtesy of Beverly Tetterton and Temple of Israel.

Wilmington, North Carolina: Temple of Israel—Sanctuary interior of the present temple, 2016; Courtesy of Beverly Tetterton and Temple of Israel.

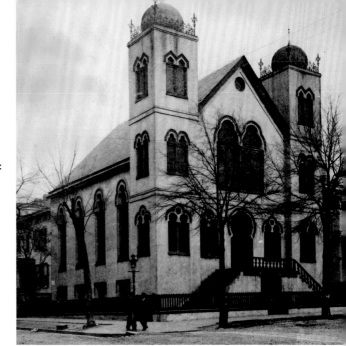

Right: Wilmington, North Carolina: Temple of Israel—Vintage print image of the present temple, 1895; Courtesy of the New Hanover Public Library and Temple of Israel.

Below: Wilmington, North Carolina: Temple of Israel—Sanctuary interior of the present temple with Rabbi Samuel Mendelssohn, ca. 1883; Courtesy of Beverly Tetterton and Temple of Israel.

NORTH DAKOTA

B'nai Israel Synagogue

The first Jewish settlers to North Dakota came during the last half of the 19th century. Many of the Jews who settled in North Dakota were farmers. Jewish farms were started across the state and small communities of Jews began to develop with informal synagogues and small cemeteries. Jews also settled in small towns of the state and they, too, held informal religious services and later formalized their organizations.

The oldest Jewish congregation is found in Grand Forks. Informal celebrations and services were held early on and, in 1891, the community welcomed the first rabbi in North Dakota. Rabbi Benjamin Papermaster, from Lithuania, initiated steps to incorporate the congregation. In 1891, the Congregation of the Children of Israel was formally organized and a site for a synagogue was selected at Girard Street and 2nd Avenue, South. The building was a distinguished frame structure. The first services in the new building were held on Rosh Hashanah 1892. Until 1906, it was the only synagogue in the territory. The Jewish community of Grand Forks grew due to the healthy economy of the city. As a result of the growth, a number of Jewish fraternal and service organizations were formed and, in 1902, a small religious school building was erected.

The current synagogue on Cottonwood Street was constructed in 1937 and is designed in the Art Deco/Streamline Moderne style. The exterior is smooth white stucco with three rounded arch doorways. The interior contains a sanctuary, small balcony area, a social hall and classrooms. A wooden ark from another congregation that merged with B'nai Israel is located in a classroom that has been used for daily services. It was sometime shortly after the move to this new building that the congregation adopted the name B'nai Israel. The B'nai Israel Montefiore Cemetery is at Gateway Drive and Columbia Road and was established in 1888.

Grand Forks, North Dakota: B'nai Israel Synagogue—Exterior of the first temple on Girard Street, n.d.; Courtesy of Bert Garwood and B'nai Israel Synagogue.

Above: Grand Forks, North Dakota: B'nai Israel Synagogue—Exterior of the present synagogue, n.d.; Courtesy of Bert Garwood and B'nai Israel Synagogue.

Below: Grand Forks, North Dakota: B'nai Israel Synagogue—Sanctuary interior of the present temple, n.d.; Courtesy of Bert Garwood and B'nai Israel Synagogue.

OHIO

Bene Israel Congregation—The Rockdale Temple

Kahal Kodesh Bene Israel was founded Cincinnati in 1824, chartered in 1830, and is the oldest Jewish congregation west of the Allegheny Mountains. The congregation was at that time of formation the only Jewish congregation within 500 miles of Cincinnati. Originally Orthodox, the congregation was actively involved in the beginnings of the Reform movement in American Judaism.

The first synagogue was dedicated in 1836 at Broadway and Sixth. The congregation and community grew rapidly and, by 1852, a new Spanish style building was dedicated on the same site. In 1869, the congregation moved into a third synagogue at Eighth and Mound Streets. As the congregation continued to grow, a rapid population shift occurred. Responding to this change and the need for additional space, Bene Israel built its fourth house of worship at Rockdale and Harvey Avenues in 1906. This Classical Revival structure, the "Rockdale Temple," was a landmark in use for 63 years. To accommodate more growth, an annex to the temple, Philipson Hall, was dedicated in 1917.

By the early 1950s, most of the congregation's membership had begun moving away from the neighborhood. A gift of property at Cross-County Highway and Ridge 100 Road was made in 1964 and, in 1967, ground was broken for the new temple. Dedicated in 1969 the temple complex contains a main chapel, outdoor courtyard/chapel, administrative wing, library, auditorium and religious school. The main chapel is a six-sided structure sheathed in translucent marble. The roof has twelve pyramid shaped skylights that form a Star of David. Renovations and an expansion were recently completed.

The first cemetery was established in 1821 downtown at Chestnut Street and Central Avenue. In 1850, the congregation established a cemetery in Walnut Hills. In 1854 B'ne Jeshurun Congregation united with the Rockdale Temple and since that time, the cemetery has been known as the United Jewish Cemetery located at 3400 Montgomery Road.

Cincinnati, Ohio: Rockdale Temple-K.K. Bene Israel— Sketch of the first synagogue at Broadway & Sixth Street, n.d.; Courtesy of Author's Collection.

Right: Cincinnati, Ohio: Rockdale Temple-K.K. Bene Israel—exterior of the new synagogue at Broadway & Sixth Street replacing the original one, pre-1979; Courtesy of CincinnatiViews.net.

Below: Cincinnati, Ohio: Rockdale Temple-K.K. Bene Israel—Vintage postcard of the Rockdale Temple, ca. 1910; Courtesy of Special Collections, College of Charleston Libraries.

ewish Synagogue,
ckdale & Harvey Aves.
Avondale, Cincinnati, O.

Above: Cincinnati, Ohio: Rockdale Temple-K.K. Bene Israel—Exterior of the present temple complex before renovations/additions, ca. 1994; Courtesy of the Author's Collection.

Below: Cincinnati, Ohio: Rockdale Temple-K.K. Bene Israel—Sanctuary interior and Ark of the present temple, 2007; Courtesy of K.K. Bene Israel.

OKLAHOMA

Temple B'nai Israel

Organized Jewish life in what is now Oklahoma was relatively late in coming. Jewish settlers began arriving in during the period following the Civil War and settled on unassigned public lands and territory to which Native Americans held title.

The first Jewish congregation began in Ardmore in 1899. Temple Emeth lasted until 2004 when the lack of Jewish residents in Ardmore necessitated closing. Their 1952 synagogue on Stanley Street still stands, as does the Mount Zion Cemetery.

By 1889 the population of Oklahoma City was 4,000 people, including ten Jewish men. High Holy Day services were held as early as 1890. By the early 20th century, the Oklahoma City Jewish community began to formally organize. The Hebrew Cemetery Association of Oklahoma City was incorporated in July 1901 and land was purchased in Fairlawn Cemetery. Temple B'nai Israel was organized in 1903 as a Reform congregation.

The cornerstone for the first house of worship at 50 Broadway Circle was laid in 1907, the year Oklahoma became the 46th state. The Oklahoma City oil boom drew growing numbers of Jews to the city. Membership had increased dramatically by 1926 and the building was becoming overcrowded. That year ground was broken for an adjoining Temple Center to house the Sunday School, the kitchen, the Temple office, a lounge and an auditorium. By 1951, Temple B'nai Israel was again in need of more space. Land for a new building at 4901 North Pennsylvania was given by Erna Krouch and her brother Julius with Norman Berlowitz donating his architecture services.

Ground was broken in 1954 and Temple B'nai Israel was dedicated in 1955. Additional Sunday School rooms and Krouch Hall were added in 1962. The temple complex also includes a large gymnasium (2000) and chapel addition (2004).

A unique aspect of B'nai Israel is the existence of the oldest continuously operating preschool in Oklahoma City, begun four years before Oklahoma Statehood. Erna Krouch immigrated from Germany to Oklahoma as a child in 1902. Ms. Krouch became a pioneer proponent of early childhood education. When the temple moved to their new building in 1955, the preschool was named after Erna Krouch and is now one of the top preschools in the city.

Oklahoma City, Oklahoma: Temple B'nai Israel—Vintage postcard of the Broadway Circle temple, n.d.; Courtesy of Special Collections, College of Charleston Libraries.

Oklahoma City, Oklahoma: Temple B'nai Israel—Exterior of the present temple, 2016; Courtesy of Temple B'nai Israel and Andrew Feiler Photography.

Oklahoma City, Oklahoma: Temple B'nai Israel—Interior of the main sanctuary of the present temple, 2016; Courtesy of Temple B'nai Israel and Andrew Feiler Photography.

Oklahoma City, Oklahoma: Temple B'nai Israel—Interior of the chapel of the present temple, 2016; Courtesy of Temple B'nai Israel and Andrew Feiler Photography.

OREGON

Temple Beth Israel

The first Jewish settlers began arriving in Oregon around the time of the California Gold Rush of 1849. The oldest Jewish congregation in the state, as well as the Pacific Northwest, is found in Portland. Temple Beth Israel was organized in 1858, just one year before Oregon statehood.

In 1861, the congregation erected the first synagogue in the state. The building was a frame structure designed in the Gothic style and was located at Fifth and Oak Streets. In 1888 Temple Beth Israel built its second house of worship at 12th and Main Streets. Designed with both Gothic and Moorish influences with twin towers, the building was used until December 1923, when it was completely destroyed by fire.

The current temple was completed in 1928 and is a fine example of the Byzantine Revival style popular with synagogue architects at the time. It is said to have been inspired by the Steelerstraße synagogue in Essen, Germany. Beth Israel's temple has a main dome and several smaller ones that are all covered with handmade terra-cotta tiles. Interior materials include stucco, plaster, wood, marble and terrazzo. Beautiful stained glass windows are to be found throughout the sanctuary.

The complex, located on wooded grounds, includes the main temple, the Sherman Educational Center (1948/1994), Harris Hall (1957) and the Schnitzer Family Center (1993). Temple Beth Israel's main building today is virtually the same as when it was first constructed. Only minor changes have taken place and great care has been given to the structure and its architectural integrity. It is listed on the National Register of Historic Places and is a City Landmark.

The Beth Israel Cemetery & Mausoleum, founded in 1857, is at 426 Southwest Taylors Ferry Road in Portland.

Above: Portland, Oregon: Congregation Beth Israel— Exterior of the first temple at Fifth and Oak Streets, n.d.; Courtesy of Congregation Beth Israel, Henry Kunowski and Oregon Historical Society.

Right: Portland, Oregon: Congregation Beth Israel— Vintage postcard of the Main and 12th Street temple, n.d.; Courtesy of the Author's Collection.

2290 – TEMPLE BETH ISRAEL, PORTLAND, OREGON.

Portland, Oregon: Congregation Beth Israel—Exterior of the present synagogue, 2013; Courtesy of Flickr User: Patrick M.

Portland, Oregon: Congregation Beth Israel—Sanctuary interior of the present synagogue, 2016; Courtesy of Congregation Beth Israel.

PENNSYLVANIA

Mikveh Israel—Synagogue of the American Revolution

Jews settled in Pennsylvania in large numbers during the first half of the 18th century, and settlement took place largely in Philadelphia and Lancaster. Pennsylvania's first and oldest Jewish congregation, Mikveh Israel, is located in the city of Philadelphia. It was founded in 1740 and formally organized in 1782. Mikveh Israel's early members were many well-known American patriots and public figures.

Mikveh Israel has worshiped in five synagogues. The first synagogue was built in 1782 at 3rd Street and Cherry Alley. A second, larger synagogue designed by architect William Strickland was built on the same site in 1825. The third building was located at 7th and Arch Streets and was designed by the same architect who designed the Philadelphia City Hall. This new synagogue was dedicated in 1860. The congregation constructed its fourth building at Broad and York Streets in 1909. This Classical style synagogue just north of Center City still stands. It was in use until the 1960s and looks much as it did when it was dedicated.

The present synagogue was dedicated in 1976 and is less than three blocks away from the site of the congregation's first synagogue. The red brick synagogue is designed in a modern and functional style and the interior of the synagogue contains architectural and ritual items from previous locations. Of special note is the reader's platform which is of Italian Marble and dates to the 1860 building. The free-standing Ark is made of oak and is silhouetted by light from the skylights above.

The congregation maintains an archive including many historic documents. Mikveh Israel, founded as a Sephardic congregation, today maintains the Sephardic form of liturgy. The membership includes members of both Sephardic and Ashkenazic origin.

Mikveh Israel maintains three cemeteries in Philadelphia. The first cemetery is a historical landmark on Spruce Street between 8th and 9th Streets in the Society Hill area. This cemetery was established in 1740 and is the burial place of over 30 Revolutionary War soldiers. The Spruce Street Cemetery, as it is known, is enclosed by a brick wall and has wrought iron gates at the entrance and a historical marker. The second cemetery located at 1114 Federal Street in South Philadelphia was established in 1841. The third and current cemetery, established in 1850, is located at 55th and Market Streets in West Philadelphia.

Above: Philadelphia, Pennsylvania: Congregation Mikveh Israel—Sketch of the first synagogue at 3rd and Cherry Street, 1984; Courtesy of Congregation Mikveh Israel and Laura Simeone, artist.

Left: Philadelphia, Pennsylvania: Congregation Mikveh Israel—Sketch of the interior of the first synagogue at 3rd and Cherry Street, 1984; Courtesy of Congregation Mikveh Israel and Laura Simeone, artist.

Above left: Philadelphia, Pennsylvania: Congregation Mikveh Israel—Sketch of the exterior of the second Cherry Street synagogue, n.d.; Courtesy of Congregation Mikveh Israel (R. Wischnitzer, *Synagogue Architecture in the United States*, 1955).

Above right: Philadelphia, Pennsylvania: Congregation Mikveh Israel—Stylized sketch of the interior of the second Cherry Street synagogue, 1845; Courtesy of Congregation Mikveh Israel (Bookplate of Mikveh Israel Rabbi Leon H. Elmaleh 1898-1927).

Right: Philadelphia, Pennsylvania: Congregation Mikveh Israel—A Jewish New Year card featuring the exterior of the 7th & Arch Streets synagogue, 1907; Courtesy of Congregation Mikveh Israel and Louis Kessler.

Above: Philadelphia, Pennsylvania: Congregation Mikveh Israel—Souvenir photograph of the sanctuary interior of the 7th & Arch Streets synagogue, 1909; Courtesy of Congregation Mikveh Israel and Louis Kessler.

Below: Philadelphia, Pennsylvania: Congregation Mikveh Israel—Exterior of the Broad Street synagogue, 1925; Courtesy of PhillyHistory.org & Philadelphia Department of Records.

Philadelphia, Pennsylvania: Congregation Mikveh Israel—Exterior of the present synagogue, 1995; Courtesy of the Author's Collection.

Philadelphia, Pennsylvania: Congregation Mikveh Israel—Sanctuary view towards the Ark, 2016; Courtesy of Congregation Mikveh Israel and Louis Kessler.

PUERTO RICO

Shaare Zedeck Congregation-Jewish Community Center

Jews were officially barred from Spanish-controlled Puerto Rico throughout much of its history. Despite this, Secret Jews may have come with Christopher Columbus to the island in the 15th century and a few other Jews came in the 19th century. During the Spanish-American War, many Jewish American servicemen gathered in Ponce together with local Jews to hold religious services. In 1898 the war ended, the island became a territory of the United States, and a few American Jews settled there. A large number of Jews fleeing Nazi Germany settled in Puerto Rico in the 1930s and 1940s. Jews also came to the island in the 1950s and 1960s fleeing the regime of Castro in Cuba. In 1952, Puerto Rico attained United States Commonwealth status.

The present-day Shaare Zedeck Congregation-Jewish Community Center of Puerto Rico traces its beginnings to 1937 when 26 Jewish families began gathering together to discuss how to best organize. In 1942, the Jewish community grew to 35 families and the Jewish Community Center was formally organized to promote social services, social activities and mutual help. In 1953, the former William Korber mansion at 903 Ponce de Leon Avenue, designed by Czech architect Antonin Nechodoma, was purchased and remodeled for use as a synagogue. Now with a permanent home, a formal congregation was born and the name Shaare Zedeck was chosen in memorial to the first synagogue destroyed by the Nazi's in Leipzig. In the 1960s additional classrooms and a large social hall were added. The congregation is the oldest of three Jewish congregations on the island, the largest one in the Caribbean. It is a member of the Conservative movement.

San Juan, Puerto Rico: Shaare Zedeck Congregation-Jewish Community Center—Exterior of the present synagogue and community center, n.d.; Courtesy of Louis Davidson Synagogues360.com

RHODE ISLAND

Touro Synagogue—Jeshuat Israel Congregation

Jews settled in Rhode Island as early as 1658 due to the religious liberty afforded residents by its founder Roger Williams. It was that year that the Jeshuat Israel Congregation was founded by Sephardic Jews who had arrived from the British West Indies colony of Barbados. Land was purchased for a cemetery in 1677, making it the oldest existing Jewish cemetery in the United States.

Groundbreaking for the first synagogue was in 1759. Noted American architect Peter Harrison was commissioned to design the building dedicated in 1763. It is the oldest existing synagogue structure in the United States. The plan of the building follows the Sephardic ritual and bears a resemblance to both the Spanish and Portuguese Synagogue of Amsterdam of 1675, and the Bevis Marks Synagogue of London built in 1701. The exterior is similar to many of the Congregational Meeting Houses of early 18th century America.

The interior of the synagogue contains a women's gallery supported by twelve Ionic and Corinthian columns, a built-in Ark, a central reading platform, and beautiful brass chandeliers. Historic ceremonial and ritual objects are located throughout the synagogue. Attached to the synagogue is an annex that once housed the Hebrew School. Patriots' Park, a newly developed area in front of the synagogue, contains a bronze reproduction of the letter sent by President George Washington to the six Jewish congregations in early America, reminding them of the basic principles of religious freedom in the new nation.

The synagogue was named for Isaac de Touro who came to Newport from Amsterdam in 1758 and was the congregation's first rabbinic leader. The synagogue is officially owned by Shearith Israel Congregation of New York City and was declared a National Historic Site in 1947, one of the earliest religious structures to be placed on the historic register.

The congregational cemetery is on Bellevue Avenue and was established in 1677. It is the burial place of many distinguished early American Jews.

Above: Newport, Rhode Island: Touro Synagogue-Congregation Jeshuat Israel—Exterior of the synagogue, 1971; Courtesy of the Library of Congress Prints & Photographs Division, HABS, RI,3-NEWP,29–1

Below left: Newport, Rhode Island: Touro Synagogue-Congregation Jeshuat Israel—Sanctuary interior of the synagogue, 1937; Courtesy of the Library of Congress Prints & Photographs Division, HABS, RI,3-NEWP,29--10 Photographer: Arthur W. LeBoeuf

Below right: Newport, Rhode Island: Touro Synagogue-Congregation Jeshuat Israel—Vintage postcard of the exterior and interior of the synagogue, ca. 1940's; Courtesy of the Author's Collection.

SOUTH CAROLINA

Kahal Kadosh Beth Elohim

Jews have lived in Charleston since the late 17th century, attracted by the colony's civil and religious liberty and economic opportunities. Jewish residents increased steadily and by 1749, the first Jewish congregation in South Carolina, Kahal Kadosh Beth Elohim was formed. The congregation was incorporated in 1791 when the 1790 state Constitution allowed for incorporation and religious freedom.

The congregation dedicated its first house of worship in 1794 on Hassell Street. This Georgian style synagogue was an extremely spacious and elegant building. A historic 1838 painting hangs in the present temple depicting the interior of the first synagogue, painted from memory by Solomon N. Carvalho when he attended the synagogue as a child.

Beth Elohim began using the Sephardic Orthodox liturgy. By the 1830s the liberalization of the religious service began and, in 1841, Beth Elohim became the first Reform congregation in the country. It was one of the founding members of the present Union for Reform Judaism. The original Hasell Street synagogue was used until April 1838 when fire destroyed the entire structure. A new synagogue was constructed on the same site and dedicated in 1841. Beth Elohim's Greek Revival synagogue is the second oldest extant synagogue in the country and the oldest in continuous use. It was designated a National Historic Landmark in 1980.

A number of relics from the 1794 synagogue were incorporated in the present building. These include the dedication stone and cornerstone, a surviving Hasell Street wall and the wrought-iron grill along Hasell Street. The interior is dominated by the large curved ark constructed of dark mahogany. The sanctuary contains stained glass windows and a domed ceiling. The Pearlstine Family Building (1950/2003) houses the religious school; social hall; the Archives Museum; offices, a library and the archives repository. The Heyman Building, an 18th century residence, houses a youth lounge and additional classroom and meeting space.

The first cemetery of the congregation is at 189 Coming Street and was established in 1762. It is a historic landmark and one of the oldest Jewish cemeteries in the United States. It is the largest Colonial Jewish burial ground and contains the graves of soldiers from the Revolutionary War, the War of 1812, and the Civil War. The DaCosta Cemetery or "Hanover Street Cemetery" at Hanover and Amherst Streets became the property of the congregation in 1847. Current burials at Beth Elohim are in the Huguenin Avenue Cemetery established in 1867.

Above: Charleston, South Carolina: Kahal Kadosh Beth Elohim—Sketch of the original synagogue based on the original by John Rubens Smith (*John Rubens Smith Collection Library of Congress*), ca. 1812; Courtesy of SeaofLiberty.org

Below left: Charleston, South Carolina: Kahal Kadosh Beth Elohim—Painting of the sanctuary interior of the original synagogue by Solomon Carvalho, 1838; Courtesy of Special Collections, College of Charleston Libraries.

Below right: Charleston, South Carolina: Kahal Kadosh Beth Elohim—View of the Ark and bimah in the present synagogue, n.d.; Courtesy of Library of Congress, Prints & Photographs Division, HABS, SC,10-CHAR,41--18

Charleston, South Carolina: Kahal Kadosh Beth Elohim—Sanctuary interior of the present synagogue, 1963, Courtesy of Library of Congress, Prints & Photographs Division, HABS, SC,10-CHAR,41–6, Photographer: Louis I. Schwartz.

Charleston, South Carolina: Kahal Kadosh Beth Elohim—Vintage postcard of the present synagogue, ca. 1970; Courtesy of the Author's Collection.

SOUTH DAKOTA

Mount Zion Temple

South Dakota's first Jewish community was established in Deadwood. The oldest Jewish cemetery in the Dakotas, Deadwood's Mount Zion Cemetery, was formed in 1892 and is part of the Mount Moriah Cemetery. The Jews of Deadwood met informally and never had a building and probably did not formalize the group. By the 1950s the group had disbanded.

Mount Zion Congregation in Sioux Falls is considered to be the oldest existing Jewish congregation in the state. Jews began settling in Sioux Falls before statehood in 1889. One of the first official acts was to provide for a cemetery. The Mount Zion Cemetery Association was incorporated in1903. About the same time, Orthodox Jews from Eastern Europe began settling in the city and, by 1909, they formed an informal group. The two groups met separately and sporadically over the years and, by 1916, a merger of the two groups was achieved. The group was incorporated under the name Congregation Sons of Israel and purchased a former church in 1916. It was the first synagogue building dedicated in South Dakota. Sons of Israel disbanded in 1973.

Differences regarding ritual and practice remained and, in 1919, a group of individuals met to form an official Reform congregation. By November of that year, the new congregation became an official member of the Reform movement. Religious services were held in a rented church until 1924 when another church was bought at 523 West 14th Street for use as a synagogue. It was remodeled and dedicated in 1926. The basement social hall and kitchen was added in 1951 and a religious school annex was added in 1958. The congregation holds a Czech Torah scroll from the Pinkas Synagogue in Prague (part of the collection of the Memorial Scrolls Trust of Torah scrolls saved in Prague during the Holocaust) and also the historic *Deadwood Torah*.

The cemetery of the congregation is the Mount Zion Cemetery stemming from the original Reform group and is located just east of the Mount Pleasant Cemetery on East 12th Street.

Sioux Falls, South Dakota: Mount Zion Temple— Exterior of the present temple, 2007; Courtesy of the Author's Collection.

TENNESSEE

Temple Israel

The 1830s and 1840s witnessed the arrival of the first Jewish wave of Jewish settlers to Tennessee. The first Jewish congregation in the state was founded in 1851 in Bolivar, but lasted only a few years. The oldest existing Jewish congregation is in Memphis. Temple Israel was formed in 1853 as B'nai Israel Congregation - Children of Israel and chartered in 1854.

Their first synagogue was dedicated in 1858 at Main and Exchange and was the first permanent synagogue in the state. By 1860, B'nai Israel Congregation had transitioned to Reform. When the Union of American Hebrew Congregations was founded in 1873, the congregation became an early member. As the congregation grew, property on Poplar between Second and Third was purchased for a larger temple. That temple was dedicated in 1882. The congregation again built a larger temple in 1915 at Poplar and Montgomery. The eclectic style building had twin towers topped by small domes and a main large dome. A modern school annex was added in 1950.

The Poplar/Montgomery temple served until 1976 when the congregation relocated to Massey Road and built a Contemporary style sanctuary and temple complex. Temple Israel features a semicircular Sanctuary and Ark with beautiful stained glass windows. The complex contains an amphitheater, a social hall, classrooms and offices, museum, archives, library, youth building and chapel. The chapel houses the Ark doors, Eternal Light and Tablets taken from the former Poplar/Montgomery Sanctuary.

The Temple Israel Cemetery (1885) is at 1708 Hernando Road. Graves from the first 1846 cemetery on Bass Avenue (later Jefferson Avenue) were moved to a special section of the Hernando Road cemetery.

Memphis, Tennessee: Temple Israel—Entrance and partial facade of the present temple, 2007; Courtesy of Lynn Franklin.

Memphis, Tennessee: Temple Israel—Sanctuary exterior of the present temple, 2007; Courtesy of Lynn Franklin.

Above: Memphis, Tennessee: Temple Israel—Sanctuary interior of the present temple, n.d.; Courtesy of Temple Israel Archives.

Below: Memphis, Tennessee: Temple Israel—Vintage postcard of the Poplar & Montgomery temple, ca. 1916; Courtesy of Special Collections, College of Charleston Libraries.

Above: Memphis, Tennessee: Temple Israel—Sanctuary interior of the Poplar Avenue & Montgomery Street temple, n.d.; Courtesy of Temple Israel Archives

Left: Memphis, Tennessee: Temple Israel—Sanctuary interior of the Poplar Avenue & Second Street temple, n.d.; Courtesy of Temple Israel Archives.

TEXAS

Congregation Beth Israel

The first and oldest Jewish congregation in the state is to be found in the city of Houston. In 1844, a small group of Jewish settlers established a Jewish cemetery in the city. This is considered to be the early beginnings of Congregation Beth Israel formed in 1854 as an Orthodox congregation and chartered in 1859.

It was not until 1874 that a purpose-built synagogue was built at Crawford and Franklin Streets. Another new synagogue at Crawford and Lamar Streets was built in 1908. After World War One, continued growth necessitated a new synagogue, which was dedicated in 1925 at Holman Avenue and Austin Street. This Classical Revival structure served until 1967 when the present new sanctuary and temple complex on North Braeswood Boulevard was dedicated. The former building on Holman Avenue now serves as part of the Houston Community College as a theater and is an official National Historic Landmark.

The present temple complex in the Meyerland section of Houston contains a large main sanctuary, a small chapel, a religious school wing, two libraries, social hall, exhibition gallery, and offices. Over the years, the facilities have been expanded and enhanced. A complete renovation of the present Sanctuary was completed in January 2017.

The original cemetery of Congregation Beth Israel was established in 1844 at 1207 West Dallas Street. Subsequent cemeteries were established at Woodlawn Cemetery as the Beth Israel Section and the Beth Israel Cemetery at 1105 Antoine Street.

Houston, Texas: Congregation Beth Israel—Vintage image of the first temple at Crawford and Franklin Streets, n.d.; Courtesy of Congregation Beth Israel Library.

Houston, Texas: Congregation Beth Israel—Vintage postcard of the Crawford and Lamar Streets temple, 1911; Courtesy of Special Collections, College of Charleston Libraries.

Houston, Texas: Congregation Beth Israel—Architectural rendering by Charles H. Boelsen of the former Holman Avenue temple to be renovated as a performing arts center, ca. 1982; Courtesy of Congregation Beth Israel Library.

Houston, Texas: Congregation Beth Israel—Exterior of the present Meyerland temple; 2016; Courtesy of Congregation Beth Israel and Judy Weidman.

Above left: Houston, Texas: Congregation Beth Israel—Close-up of the Ark in the present Meyerland temple, ca. 1990's; Courtesy of Congregation Beth Israel.

Above right: Houston, Texas: Congregation Beth Israel—View of the new Ark and bimah in the present Meyerland temple, 2017; Courtesy of Congregation Beth Israel and Judy Weidman

UNITED STATES VIRGIN ISLANDS

The Hebrew Congregation of St. Thomas

The Hebrew Congregation of St. Thomas in Charlotte Amalie was established in 1796 primarily by descendants of Spanish Jews who had fled Spain's Inquisition. They had ties to England, Denmark, France, Germany and Holland and followed the Dutch and English who settled various Caribbean islands. The first synagogue was built in 1803 and destroyed by fire in 1804. The partially rebuilt synagogue burned down again in 1806. In 1813, a building on new property was used until 1823 when it was dismantled and a new synagogue was built on the same site on Crystal Gade on Synagogue Hill. Destroyed again by fire in 1831, the present synagogue was built in 1833. The Torah scrolls and eternal light from the 1831 building were saved and many furnishings in the sanctuary date to the 1833 building. The synagogue was restored in 2000.

The synagogue is the oldest in use under the American flag and the 2nd oldest synagogue in the western hemisphere. In 1917, Denmark ratified a treaty to sell the Danish West Indies to the United States for 25 million in gold coin. The congregation, originally Orthodox, followed the Sephardic liturgy, but has been affiliated with the Reform movement for many years. In homage to the roots of the congregation, there is a sand floor and the pews face one another rather than the bimah. A small museum was added in 1996. The synagogue is a major tourist destination and active congregation and maintains two Jewish cemeteries on the island.

Charlotte Amalie, St. Thomas United States Virgin Islands: Hebrew Congregation of St. Thomas— Annex building and entrance to the Sanctuary, 2012; Courtesy of Author's Collection.

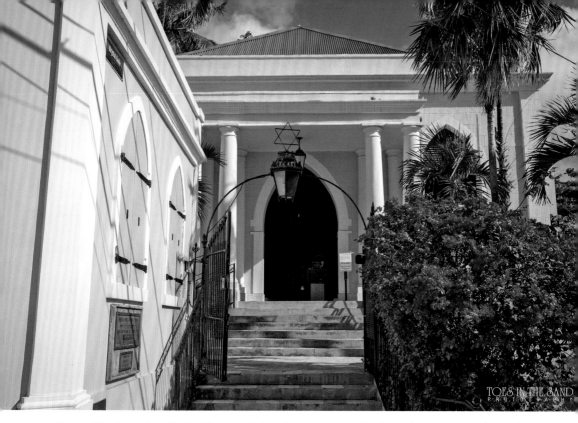

Above: Charlotte Amalie, St. Thomas United States Virgin Islands: Hebrew Congregation of St. Thomas—Sanctuary and annex exterior of the present synagogue, 2016; Courtesy of Michael Garcia and Toes In The Sand Photography.

Below: Charlotte Amalie, St. Thomas United States Virgin Islands: Hebrew Congregation of St. Thomas—Sanctuary interior of the present synagogue, 2016; Courtesy of Michael Garcia and Toes In The Sand Photography.

UTAH

Congregation Kol Ami

The first Jewish organization in Utah, a Hebrew benevolent society, was established in Salt Lake City in 1864. The oldest existing Jewish congregation in Utah is Congregation Kol Ami in Salt Lake City. It came into being in 1972 through the merger of two historic Salt Lake congregations: B'nai Israel and Montefiore.

B'nai Israel was established in 1873 as an Orthodox congregation and incorporated in 1881. Their first synagogue was dedicated in 1883 at First West and Third South. By 1885, the congregation had fully embraced the Reform style of service. A larger synagogue was dedicated in 1891 at 249 South Fourth East. The Romanesque Revival style building was reportedly based on Berlin's Fasanenstraße Synagogue as most of the founders were German by birth. The temple was in use until 1976 and is listed on the National Register of Historic Places.

The second congregation, Montefiore, began informally around 1885 as a breakaway group. Its founders were primarily Eastern European Jews who preferred the Orthodox worship ritual. Montefiore was officially organized in 1899 and later joined the Conservative movement of Judaism. Congregation Montefiore dedicated its first and only synagogue in 1903 at 355 South Third East. The structure has twin domed towers and is designed in the Moorish Revival style. It was in use until 1976 and is now used as a church and a designated Historic Landmark.

In 1969, the religious schools of B'nai Israel and Montefiore merged. In 1972, the articles of consolidation were signed, resulting in a new congregation named Kol Ami, or All of My People. Since most of the Jewish community no longer lived near either of the two synagogue buildings, a Contemporary synagogue was built at 2425 East Heritage Way. The building was first occupied for the High Holy Day services of 1976. The Contemporary building contains a sanctuary, chapel, social hall, classrooms and a library. The congregation is affiliated with both the Reform and Conservative branches of American Judaism.

Congregation Kol Ami maintains three cemeteries: B'nai Israel Cemetery at 1011 East 4th Avenue, Montefiore Cemetery at 1085 East 4th Avenue and Shaarei Zedek Cemetery (an Orthodox congregation 1916-1940) at 915 East 11th Avenue. B'nai Israel's cemetery is the oldest in the state and served as the burial place for many early Jewish residents of Idaho, Wyoming and Nevada as this cemetery was the only one available for some time.

Above left: Salt Lake City, Utah: Congregation Kol Ami—Exterior of the former B'nai Israel Temple, 2007; Courtesy of the Author's Collection.

Above right: Salt Lake City, Utah: Congregation Kol Ami—Exterior of the former Montefiore Congregation synagogue, 2007; Courtesy of the Author's Collection, Photographer: Richard W. Clark.

Salt Lake City, Utah: Congregation Kol Ami—Exterior of the present synagogue, 2007; Courtesy of the Author's Collection.

VERMONT

Ohavi Zedek Synagogue

Vermont was the first state to enter the Union after the original thirteen colonies, but did not have a Jewish community until the latter half of the 19th century. The first congregation, B'nai Israel, was organized in Poultney in 1870, but no longer exists. The oldest existing Jewish congregation, however, is to be found in Burlington. Congregation Ohavi Zedek was founded on April 8th, 1885. Its first synagogue was built in 1885 through the physical efforts of its members and located at Hyde and Archibald Streets. In 1887, the congregation incorporated and a cemetery was established.

As the Burlington Jewish community grew, two additional congregations were formed. Chai Odom (Adam) Congregation was founded in 1889 and built a synagogue which still stands at 105 Hyde Street, and in the early 1900s Ahavath Garim Congregation was founded.

In 1939, the entire Jewish community affiliated with Ohavi Zedek Congregation and the various cemeteries and properties were combined. Ohavi Zedek began as an Orthodox congregation, but in 1950 the congregation affiliated with what is now the United Synagogue of Conservative Judaism. Their new Mid-Century Modern style synagogue was dedicated in 1952 and is thought to be one of the first synagogues to be designed by a female architect, Ruth Freeman. The 1885 synagogue was sold to the Ahavath Gerim Congregation, and is now undergoing restoration. A 1910 mural from the former Chai Adam synagogue was recently restored and moved to a permanent space in Ohavi Zedek's foyer.

Though the Jewish community of Poultney no longer exists, their cemetery is the oldest in the state. There are several historic Jewish cemeteries that have served the Burlington Jewish Community since 1887.

Right: Burlington, Vermont—Ohavi Zedek Synagogue—Exterior of the original synagogue at Hyde & Archibald Streets, 2016; Courtesy of Ohavi Zedek Synagogue and Photographer: Miriam C. Mayer.

Below: Burlington, Vermont—Ohavi Zedek Synagogue—Sanctuary interior of the original synagogue at Hyde & Archibald Streets, 2016; Courtesy of Ohavi Zedek Synagogue and Photographer: Miriam C. Mayer.

Above: Burlington, Vermont—Ohavi Zedek Synagogue—Exterior of the present synagogue, 2016; Courtesy of Ohavi Zedek Synagogue and Photographer: Miriam C. Mayer.

Below: Burlington, Vermont—Ohavi Zedek Synagogue—Sanctuary interior of the present synagogue, 2016; Courtesy of Ohavi Zedek Synagogue and Photographer: Miriam C. Mayer.

VIRGINIA

Congregation Beth Ahabah

Jews have lived in Virginia since the mid-1600s, but because of political, religious and economic disadvantages, the community did not organize early on. Virginia was one of the last of the thirteen colonies to establish an organized Jewish community. The oldest existing Jewish congregation is Beth Ahabah in Richmond founded in 1841. The congregation connects its beginnings to Kahal Kadosh Beth Shalome, established in Richmond in 1789. When Beth Shalome was founded, it was the sixth Jewish congregation in the United States and followed the Orthodox Sephardic ritual. Beth Shalome built the first synagogue in Virginia in 1822 on Mayo Street in Richmond.

During the 1830s and 1840s, German speaking Jews came to America. Many settled in Richmond because of its well-known culture and its acceptance of Jews in society. The new immigrants founded Congregation Beth Ahabah in 1841, based on the Ashkenazic form of worship. Their first synagogue was built in 1848 at 11th and Marshall. A larger synagogue was built on the same site in 1880. In 1875, they joined the Reform movement. In 1898 Kahal Kadosh Beth Shalome formally consolidated with Congregation Beth Ahabah.

The present Classical Revival synagogue at Franklin and Ryland Streets in the historic Fan District was dedicated in 1904. The sanctuary is complete with stained glass windows (including a Tiffany Studios window), an original organ from Germany and a large dome. The complex also contains a chapel, a religious school building and offices. An archives and museum was established in 1977 and their adjacent building was dedicated in 1983.

In 1791, the first Jewish cemetery in Virginia was established on Franklin Street between 20th and 21st Streets. A second cemetery was established in 1816 at 4th and Hospital Streets. The original cemetery is now a designated historic site. The cemetery at 5th and Hospital Streets contains a Confederate Soldiers Section that is believed to be the only one of its kind in an American Jewish cemetery.

Jewish Synagogue,
(Franklin and Ryland St.), Richmond, Va.

Above: Richmond, Virginia: Congregation Beth Ahabah—Vintage postcard of the present synagogue, ca. 1912; Courtesy of the Author's Collection.

Below: Richmond, Virginia: Congregation Beth Ahabah—Sanctuary interior of the present synagogue, n.d.; Courtesy of Beth Ahabah Museum & Archives, Chuck Savage, photographer.

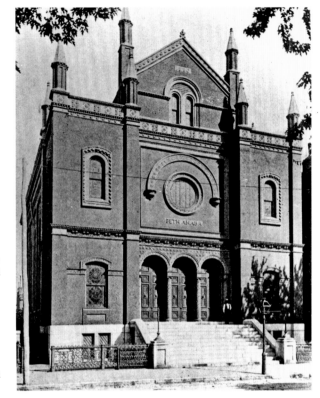

Right: Richmond, Virginia:
Congregation Beth Ahabah—
Exterior of the second synagogue
built at 11th and Marshall Streets,
Courtesy of Beth Ahabah Museum
& Archives.

Below: Richmond, Virginia:
Congregation Beth Ahabah—
Exterior of the first synagogue
(Beth Shalome) in Virginia, n.d.;
Courtesy of Beth Ahabah Museum
& Archives.

WASHINGTON STATE

Temple Beth Shalom

A Latvian adventurer, Adolph Friedman, who came to Washington in the late 1840s, is considered the first Jew to have settled in the territory. By 1889, when Washington became the 42nd state, Jews had been contributing to the state's economy and growth for four decades.

The first Jewish congregation, Ohaveth Sholom, was established in Seattle in 1889 and built a synagogue in 1892, but the congregation disbanded in 1895. The oldest existing Jewish congregation is Temple Shalom in Spokane founded in 1890 as Congregation Emanu-El. In 1891, fundraising began to build a house of worship at 3rd Avenue and Madison Street. The small frame building was dedicated on September 14, 1892, and held the distinction as the first synagogue in the state, because Seattle's much larger Ohaveth Sholom wasn't dedicated until September 18, 1892.

An Orthodox congregation, Keneseth Israel Synagogue, was established in 1901 and built their synagogue in 1909 at 4th and Adams. In 1928, Emanu-El dedicated a new Classical Revival style synagogue at 8th and Walnut. The building still stands and is now a church. The two congregations merged in 1966 to become Temple Shalom, a liberal Conservative congregation. Their new synagogue was dedicated in 1968 at 30th and Perry. Stained glass and pulpit menorahs from previous buildings were saved for the new synagogue. A historical marker stands near 3rd and Madison, marking the site of the first synagogue in the state.

Spokane's Jewish cemetery, Mount Nebo, is adjacent to Greenwood Memorial Park and was initially established by Keneseth Israel. An earlier cemetery, Ahavath Israel, was established in 1914, but used infrequently and sold not long after it was dedicated.

Spokane, Washington: Temple Beth Shalom—Exterior of the former Emanu-El synagogue at 8th & Walnut Streets, 2013; Courtesy of WaymArking.com User: BK-Hunters.

Above left: Spokane, Washington: Temple Beth Shalom—Exterior of the first Emanu-El synagogue and the first synagogue in Washington State, n.d.; Courtesy of Temple Beth Shalom.

Above right: Spokane, Washington: Temple Beth Shalom—Exterior of Keneseth Israel's 4th Avenue & Adams Street synagogue, n.d.; Courtesy of Temple Beth Shalom.

Spokane, Washington: Temple Beth Shalom—Exterior of the present Temple Shalom, 2016; Courtesy of Temple Beth Shalom, Photographer: Sharon Beltz.

WEST VIRGINIA

Congregation L'Shem Shomayim—Temple Shalom

The first Jewish settlers in West Virginia probably arrived in the 1830s as the towns of Wheeling and Charleston became important trading locations. The first Jewish community was organized in Wheeling in 1849 when a Jewish cemetery association was formed. That same year Congregation L'Shem Shomayim was founded primarily by German Jews. This new congregation dedicated the state's first synagogue at 1214 Eoff Street in 1892. The Moorish Revival temple contained a dome, stained glass windows and elaborate furnishings. Unfortunately, the building no longer stands. For years, the congregation was known as the "Eoff Street Temple."

Congregation L'Shem Shomayim was organized as an Orthodox congregation, but adopted the Reform ritual and became one of the charter members of today's Union for Reform Judaism. As the congregation grew, the Eoff Street Temple became increasingly inadequate. In 1955 ground was broken at Bethany Pike and Walnut Avenue for a new synagogue known as the "Woodsdale Temple," which was dedicated in 1958.

In the 1920s the Conservative Synagogue of Israel was formed in Wheeling and built their own synagogue on Edgington Lane in 1927. In 1974, the two congregations merged to form Temple Shalom-Congregation L'Shem Shomayim. Temple Shalom continues to own their 1849 cemetery. Mount Wood Jewish Cemetery is located on the National Pike. The Synagogue of Israel Cemetery established in 1954 is also maintained by Temple Shalom.

Right: Wheeling, West Virginia: Temple Shalom—Letterhead sketch of the Eoff Street Temple, n.d. Courtesy of Temple Shalom Archives.

Opposite: Wheeling, West Virginia: Temple Shalom—Exterior of the former Synagogue of Israel on Edgington Lane, ca. 1974; Courtesy of Temple Shalom Archives.

Below: Wheeling, West Virginia: Temple Shalom—Sanctuary exterior of the present temple, 2007; Courtesy of the Author's Collection.

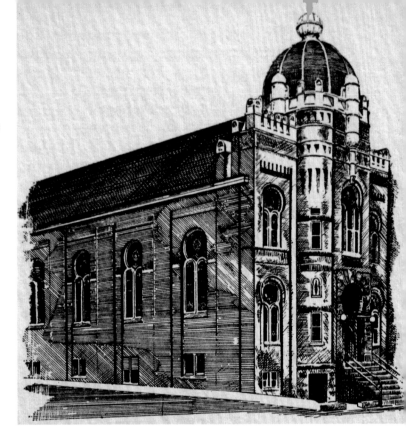

WISCONSIN

Congregation Emanu-El B'nai Jeshurun

During the 1830s, the first practicing Jews settled permanently in the village of Milwaukee. In the fall of 1847, the first Jewish religious service in Wisconsin was held and a minyan was begun. Congregation Emanu-El B'ne Jeshurun, the oldest existing congregation in the state, traces its start to that first service.

In 1850, Congregation Imanu-Al was organized. In 1856, Imanu-Al Congregation and Ahavath Emuno Congregation (1854) came together to form the Reform Congregation B'ne Jeshurun. A third congregation, Anshe Emeth (1855), merged with B'ne Jeshurun in 1859. It was at this same time that B'ne Jeshurun dedicated its first synagogue on Fourth Street near State Street. Dissidents from B'ne Jeshurun established Congregation Emanu-El in 1869 and built their first synagogue at Broadway and State in 1872. As the residential character of the area changed, Congregation Emanu-El built a large Classical style synagogue on East Kenwood Boulevard in use by 1923.

Both congregations prospered for many years. As Jews moved out of the downtown area, many moved to the area where Emanu-El built its new synagogue. When B'ne Jeshurun's location at 10th and Cedar Streets was earmarked for the new Milwaukee County Courthouse, plans began for the merger of the city's two Reform congregations. The consolidation was completed in 1927, the name, Emanu-El B'ne Jeshurun was adopted and the merged congregation began worshiping in the East Kenwood Boulevard synagogue. A plaque on the courthouse commemorates the B'ne Jeshurun synagogue.

In 1974, an Educational Building was added as part of a total renovation. The complex consisted of a sanctuary, chapel, community hall, library, religious school and offices. In 1980, an Archives Center was established. In 1997, the congregation dedicated its new building on Brown Deer Road in suburban River Hills. This became their permanent home in 2000. A renovation and expansion was completed in 2009. Phillip Katz designed the Sanctuary and artwork is by artist Toby Kahn. The former Kenwood Boulevard synagogue is now the Helen Bader Concert Hall of the University of Wisconsin-Milwaukee.

The Imanu-Al Cemetery was dedicated in 1852 at West Hopkins and West Chambers Streets (though the first burial took place in 1848). It was also known as the Hopkins Street Cemetery. This cemetery, the oldest Jewish cemetery in the state, was in use until around 1888. It is preserved and cared for by Emanu-El B'ne Jeshurun. Over the years many graves were eventually relocated from the Hopkins Street Cemetery to the present Greenwood Cemetery which was established in 1869 and adjoins the Forest Home Cemetery.

Opposite above: Milwaukee, Wisconsin: Congregation Emanu-El B'nai Jeshurun—Exterior of the Emanu-El synagogue at North Broadway and East State Street; n.d.; Courtesy of the Jewish Museum Milwaukee.

Opposite below: Milwaukee, Wisconsin: Congregation Emanu-El B'nai Jeshurun—Exterior of the 10th & Cedar Streets synagogue of B'nai Jeshurun, n.d.; Courtesy of the Jewish Museum Milwaukee.

Above: Milwaukee, Wisconsin: Congregation Emanu-El B'nai Jeshurun—Exterior of the Emanu-El B'nai Jeshurun synagogue on Kenwood Boulevard, ca. 1970's; Courtesy of the Jewish Museum Milwaukee.

Below: Milwaukee, Wisconsin: Congregation Emanu-El B'nai Jeshurun—View of the Ark and bimah in the present synagogue in River Hills, 2016; Courtesy of Wikimedia Commons User: Jennaxel.

WYOMING

Mount Sinai Congregation

The first Jewish religious services in Wyoming were held in the 1870s and the first congregation, Temple Emanu-El was incorporated in Cheyenne in 1888. This Reform congregation was an outgrowth of a sisterhood group established in 1875 and was the first Jewish organization in the state. An Orthodox congregation, Mount Sinai, was established in Cheyenne in 1910 by immigrants from Eastern and Central Europe.

In 1915, the Mount Sinai Congregation built the first synagogue in the state at 1921 Pioneer Avenue. The synagogue had a central round window with a Star of David in the facade as well as twin towers capped by small domes. The synagogue building was demolished in 1979 but a historical marker stands on the site.

By the 1920s, Temple Emanu-El either disbanded or merged with the Mount Sinai Congregation as the Jewish population in Cheyenne began to decrease. Mount Sinai Congregation built a large modern synagogue at 2610 Pioneer Avenue in 1951. There is a large sanctuary with 80 beautiful stained glass windows dedicated in 1977, and a smaller chapel as well as a library, classrooms and social hall. A unique feature is a small stream that runs through the basement of the synagogue, discovered by the contractor that now serves as a valued ritual bath of "living waters."

Mount Sinai Congregation's cemetery, established in the 1890s, is located within Cheyenne's City Cemetery.

Left: Cheyenne, Wyoming— Mt. Sinai Congregation – Sketch of the first synagogue on Pioneer Avenue, the first in the state, 1915; Courtesy of the Author's Collection (*Cheyenne State Leader* October 26, 1915).

Below: Cheyenne, Wyoming – Mt. Sinai Congregation—Exterior of the present synagogue on Pioneer Avenue, n.d.; Courtesy of Louis Davidson Synagogues360.com